NORTOPIA

jovis

EDS.: *Caroline Spliid Høgsbro & Antje Wischmann*

NORTOPIA

MODERN NORDIC ARCHITECTURE AND POSTWAR GERMANY

THE NORDIC SONDERWEG

FAREWELL WELFARE

A PROMISING FUTURE

Antje Wischmann and Caroline Spliid Høgsbro

THE OCCASION

A Nordic-Berlin Encounter

The impulse for the publication of this anthology dates back a number of years.[1] The fiftieth anniversary of "Interbau in 1957" in Berlin's Hansaviertel, celebrated in 2007, not only naturally invites a retrospective but also presents an enticing opportunity to examine a range of Nordic-German perspectives.[2] In the Nordic countries, the dawn of modernity was ushered in during the 1920s and 1930s and continued in the 1950s with a distinct ideological and sociopolitical accent. The completely new planned town was later often disparagingly compared with the "natural city" (die "gewachsene Stadt"), which embodied the ideal of classic European urbanity. However, historical continuity was precisely what was *not* aspired to in the "city of tomorrow," which was more concerned with constructed utopias and visions in the age of a crystallizing project of modernism.

1 Primary literature for this introduction: Florian Heilmeyer et al.: *Schaustelle Nachkriegsmoderne Berlin,* Berlin*: Stadtwandel Verlag, 2007,* especially pp. 17-21; Gabi Dolff-Bonekämpfer and Franziska Schmidt: *Das Hansaviertel. Internationale Nachkriegsmoderne in Berlin,* Berlin: Verlag Bauwesen, 1999; Harmut Häußermann, Dieter Läpple, Walter Siebel: *Stadtpolitik,* Frankfurt/Main: Suhrkamp, 2008; Albrecht Koschorke: "Moderne als Wunsch. Krieg und Städtebau im 20. Jahrhundert," in: *Leviathan. Zeitschrift für Sozialwissenschaft,* vol. 27, no. 1, 1998, pp. 23-42; Stefanie Schulz and Carl-Georg Schulz: *Das Hansaviertel. Ikone der Moderne,* Berlin: Braun, 2007; ibid.: "Einleitung," in: Schulz and Schulz: *Das Hansaviertel,* pp. 9-33.

2 In this volume, we define the concept of "North" as encompassing Sweden, Finland, Norway, Denmark, and Iceland, which can be viewed in a unified context in their urban development after the Second World War. The expression "Nordic Modernism" is used as a kind of label that the contributors to the volume critically address. For a more detailed discussion of the concept of "North" as a social, cultural, and political unit, see Thomas Hall: "The North – Does it Exist?," in: ibid. (ed.): *Planning and Urban Growth in the Nordic Countries,* London: E and FN SPON, 1991, pp. 1-5. In the same volume, the intensive communication and mutual inspiration among Nordic town planners in the postwar period is examined more closely. See Hall: "Is there a Nordic Planning Tradition?," pp. 257-59.

The forward-looking orientation of New Architecture, palpable up to the present day, is still acknowledged as an innovative pool of potential in architectural criticism: a progressive profiling that promises landmark architectural solutions. In the postwar period of the nascent Cold War, the building exhibition was seen as the manifestation of West Germany's democratic consolidation and its increasing international recognition. The "Interbau" could demonstrate a successful "esthetic re-education."

Constructed Models

The Hansaviertel is a paradigmatic example of the reconstruction of German cities in the postwar period and the architectural conveyance of laudable everyday life characteristic for the era of the Economic Miracle. An analogous phase of prosperity in the North is referred to as the "Record Years." The pioneering suburb of Vällingby near Stockholm (1955) – even paid tribute to by Lewis Mumford[3] – accrued a similar exemplary status to the Hansaviertel, presenting varied developments with an almost ornamental layout in an area of attractive scenery. Vällingby promised light, air, and bold design, which among others specifically meant one room for every member of the family and the latest standard of amenities – in telling contrast to the dilapidated and cramped old city areas of Stockholm from which many residents came. Vällingby represents the intact Swedish "folkhem," its urban planning the well-meaning constructed intentions of a caring state.

The diversified development appears to guarantee the positive influence of individualistic ideals, clear social emancipatory targets, and the (oft-cited) "human scale" of the architecture on the residents. During implementation of the "Million Program" (social housing) from 1965 to 1975, criticism of the technocratic nanny state was growing in Sweden and protest arose against the demolition of old buildings and town

3 Lewis Mumford: *Die Stadt. Geschichte und Ausblick,* Vol. 2, Munich: DTV, 1980 [1961], pp. 794-796.

planning oriented towards motor traffic. Monotonous urban areas on the periphery, frequently denigrated as concrete suburbs, agglomerations of tower blocks, endless pre-fabricated façades – these stereotypical images were used to define a disrespectful, inhumane style of residential architecture. The accusations of constructed monotony and repressive standardization were ultimately partially responsible for the discontinuation of tower block architecture for residential accommodation in the mid-1970s.

At the time the Hansaviertel and the Vällingby neighborhood were built, "social engineering" was not yet an ambivalent or stigmatized concept; large-scale planning was acknowledged as a "social art of engineering" in Sweden. This regulatory and disciplining potential has been examined in detail in research since the 1980s and also exploited on the basis of comparative studies, in particular of Swedish history from circa 1930.[4]

It was only with the "folkhem" crisis that the risks and questionable ideological assumptions emerged in full clarity, nearly leading to a demonization of the Stockholm suburbs constructed in the late 1960s. Similarly to the neighborhoods built in other western European countries in the context of suburbanization, they were alleged to be characterized by a lamentable lack of urbanity. Vällingby has now long been seen from a nostalgic perspective: a district with a 1950s-style kidney table contour in an intimated open-air museum atmosphere, albeit equipped with a twenty-first-century century mecca of consumerism to attract tourist shoppers.

A New Start "From Scratch"

However, one aspect of the Hansaviertel's modernist architecture, which today still seems imaginable as a liberating beginning full of possibilities, is the new start in the German postwar period of suppression and anachronism, often viewed with an infectious enthusiasm. Even the pathos initially seems understandable – the aim, after all, was to demolish a deforming system, to realize the "democratic spirit," and in

4 A representative example is: Norbert Götz: *Ungleiche Geschwister. Die Konstruktion von nationalsozialistischer Volksgemeinschaft und schwedischem Volksheim*, Baden-Baden: Nomos, 2001.

so doing provide a contrast to National Socialist architecture and also such socialist architecture as the Stalinallee in East Berlin. In a quote from the exhibition catalog *Stadt von morgen* (1959), it may seem as if the technological and mental progress of West German society had already emphatically distanced itself from its former models, so that creating an architecturally modern frame for the functional unit of the modern city-dweller collective was long overdue:

> Our cities conform least to the development of our technical world. Encrusted in obsolete urban structures, our cities remain in stony, earth-bound traditions and fail miserably in the face of the tasks our times have set. In comparison with the needs and possibilities of our technical-industrial working methods, our cities do not "work" any more.[5]

The design of the European city was characterized by its chief function as a trading center, its monocentrist overall concept, and its typical concentration on institutions of political, religious, and economic power. From the point of view of the modernist town planning pioneers inspired, among others, by Le Corbusier, this old city had simply had its day. Significantly, the building plot of the Hansaviertel and the construction material used even twelve years after the end of the war are still enriched with the experience of war, making this forward surge stand out all the more clearly as an idealistic-utopian endeavor.[6] The plot covers the old Hansaviertel, its dense *Gründerzeit* buildings almost completely destroyed in the war. Brick chippings from debris were mixed in the concrete.[7]

In the 1960s, reconceiving the city was also a task for the structuralist project of understanding all areas of life, in which the urban elements were understood as linguistically analogous units of meaning within a closed system. The esthetic effect of the

5 Karl Otto: *Stadt von morgen,* 1959; quoted in Schulz/Schulz: "Einleitung," p. 23.

6 Albrecht Koschorke even speaks of a "hatred of obsolete urban structures," (p. 38) and describes the enthusiasm for the areas destroyed in the war, quasi decontaminated, as an ambivalent attitude; many New Building architects would have interpreted the destruction of the Old City as a window of opportunity (see pp. 40-42). Koschorke links the two concepts of tabula rasa and amnesia, relating the latter in turn to ahistoricity and contempt for history (see p. 39).

7 See Schulz and Schulz: "Einleitung," p. 25.

spatial proportions of the group of buildings in the Hansaviertel, by which the tower blocks were presented as in a sculpture park, can also be imagined by today's visitors.[8] There are visual axes and structured areas that are easy to survey, or squares and paths that only gradually open up in the course of exploration. The six tower blocks are still indirectly emphasized through interconnecting low-rise construction (single-story buildings with flat roofs such as Arne Jacobsen's atrium houses). This kind of network of interactions among the buildings can also be related to the structuralist concept, as this contrast is comprehensible in the sense of a meaningful balance of vertical and horizontal orientation.

The architectural ensemble of the Hansaviertel bridges the architectural and ideological gap between the poles of "height and openness" on the one hand, and "low construction and density" on the other. This reciprocal profiling of the dwellings can be explained by the layout of the building exhibition and the according relationship of the buildings to each other.[9] The exhibition esthetics of "Interbau" additionally resemble those of trade fairs or sales shows and join the tradition of the Stockholm exhibition of 1930, the Stuttgart Building Exhibition of the German Work Federation of 1927, or the Danish exhibition "Forum" in 1929.

For the New Building movement, which is still frequently characterized as ignorant of continuity or even ahistorical in comparison with the old, value-enriched, natural European city, the authors of the volume *Stadtpolitik* (2008) compile the following features:

- In place of mixing functions, a strict division in areas for living, for working, for relaxation, and for traffic were determined; division was the declared basic prerequisite for a functioning city, public areas, places of social cohabitation no longer played any role;
- in place of mixing forms of transportation, a strict division of road traffic and pedestrians was promoted [...];

8 In particular the Dutch tower block by J.H. van der Broek and J.B. Bakema, the yellow H. Schwippert building, or the O. Niemeyer block with its elevator tower.

9 Such diversity of individual buildings as exists in the Hansaviertel is fairly rare in "uniformly planned" neighborhoods of social housing construction in the 1960s and 1970s.

- In place of the urban arterial road, the "parkway," freed from all roadside development, was conceived, running through the city solely according to the laws of flowing movement, without junctions and without direct access for local residents;
- In place of block system construction [tower block units];
- In place of the densely-built, stony city, free-standing groups of buildings in a "structured" urban landscape, which is to be set out in large-scale green spaces reflecting sunlight exposure.[10]

Well-meaning regulations, especially when combined with utopian ambitions, require exaggerated models, which inevitably involve exclusion or lead to repressive practices, and thus the educational claim of New Building results in the accusation of a patronizing attitude. The residents of the Hansaviertel could easily avoid some of this nannying (e.g. the planned use of common rooms), but not all of it (e.g., design of the usually economical kitchen dimensions for use by one person, i.e., the housewife). Certain civic models concerning both the social mobility of the employed as well as with regard to reproduction, consumption, and recreation, were, among others, formulated via town planning and architecture.

In an interview, one Hansaviertel resident who has lived in an Arne Jacobsen bungalow since 1960 describes her first visit to the new neighborhood:

> It was an island of cleanliness, and in this unusual style – it was totally new! And that was what we all longed for. I was 15 years old when the war ended. There was an enormous desire to take part in a new form of government, this democracy we were trying to acquire, the sense of departure that was everywhere. For this, we were prepared to make any sacrifice. This architectural style really absorbed me. This house is just as much mine as the clothes on my back.[11]

10 Häußermann and Läpple: *Stadtpolitik*, p. 58.

11 Caroline Spliid Høgsbro: "Jacobsen Bungalow," in: Lidia Tirri (ed.): *Wohnlabor Hansaviertel – Geschichten aus der Stadt von Morgen*, Berlin: Amberpress, 2007, pp. 28-31, p. 30.

In contrast, a slightly muted enthusiasm can be sensed in the words of Thomas Millroth, who as a child moved from a crowded working-class area of Stockholm to airy Vällingby:

> The suburb was spread out like a flower, it seemed to me, with shimmering neon names like Kvickly and Tempo at its center and the houses, the hills, the tower blocks, the bushes, and the lawns all around as petals, scented and colorful [...]. An intoxicating beauty, but so transparent.[12]

The View Northwards

A historical contextualization of housing construction and town planning in the 1950s and 1960s, to which this volume would like to contribute, is essential not only to gain critical insights from the retrospective, but also to fathom the existing present-day fascination with the phenomenon of a scheme like the Hansaviertel. One component of this is doubtless also the historical derivation of the architectural-ideological bases, which also incorporated social democratically-oriented Nordic town planning. The welfare phenomenon – the most attractive component of Nordic modernism – and housing construction were at times understood as virtual synonyms.

Probably the most appealing Nordic export of this time is the above-mentioned socially emancipatory and political belief in progress. With respect to Sweden, this central theme is defined by the "spirit of Saltsjöbaden," which aspires to a cooperation between the job market and economic policy in which both sides desire consensus in a programmatic way. In the Saltsjö agreement of 1938, trade unions and employers' representatives undertook to solve arising conflicts independently without availing themselves of state intervention. Willingness to cooperate, mutual respect, and the declared intention of negotiating peaceful solutions held the prospect of stability and harmony.

12 Thomas Millroth: *Vällingbyblues*, Stockholm: Inferi, 1984, pp. 18f. See also Antje Wischmann: "Die Entdeckung der Vorstadt," in: ibid.: *Verdichtete Stadtwahrnehmung. Untersuchungen zum literarischen und urbanistischen Diskurs in Skandinavien 1955-1995*, Berlin: Berliner Wissenschaftsverlag, 2003, pp. 343-361, pp. 350-351.

Criticism

Open construction such as is found in the Hansaviertel and Vällingby was called into question from the mid-1970s on account of its vastness and "non-density," and from that point repeatedly cited in order to denounce the anonymous, faceless city and its lack of urbanity. The functional division gained the reputation of a clinical measure inimicable to life, while the functional mixture was seen as a "natural" characteristic of the European city, whose qualities drew so many people back to city centers at the end of the 1980s. This reurbanization presented a striking trend reversal, since the centers had without exception been considered trouble areas in the 1970s and early 1980s. Criticism of functionalism thus resulted in urbanity based on the model of the natural, monocentric city appearing in a gilded light. These double standards are also good grounds for placing the neighborhoods of New Building in an appropriate light.

If the anniversary of Vällingby and the celebratory event of the Hansaviertel are considered, it is the rich array of antiquated, often biographically inspired strategies of recollection[13] that underlines the residents' growing acceptance and identification. Both locations have become memory spaces: in the parallel lines of urban and personal biographical development, an attachment to place is expressed, which was previously reserved for time-honored urban locations or rural regions. In the manner of outsourced self-reflection, the residents still direct their interest at the Hansaviertel or Vällingby after having left these estate areas of childhood and youth – suburbs in the esthetic of New Building are now themselves distinct places whose wealth of sensual perception is no longer in question.

13 Marian Engel: *Leben in der Stadt von morgen. 50 Jahre Berliner Hansaviertel*, Berlin: Stadt von morgen, 2007; Svenska Bostäder: *Vällingby – från Centrum till City*, Stockholm: Anders Hanser Produktion, 2008.

THE ESSAYS IN THIS VOLUME

The Nordic countries had become a "place of pilgrimage for international planners" in the 1950s:

> "[T]he North had proved receptive to ideas prevalent at the time and [...] it had the opportunity to realize them – which it did with considerable architectural skill – before England's New Town program had really started to take shape."[14]

Universal interest in the Nordic welfare model boosted existing interest in housing construction in the North,[15] and one possible explanation for the exemplary character of this Nordic model for industrialized democratic societies may subsist in the so-called "predogmatic reality of knowledge,"[16] presenting "a corrective to the value-nihilist, utilitarian dimension of welfare politics."[17] In chapter 3, entitled "The Nordic Way to Modernity," Bernd Hennigsen, for example, describes a number of distinct cultural historical substructures which have shaped the Nordic countries' path to modern industrialized society. The architecture of housing and city construction presents a materialization of civic and socioeconomic guiding principles.

With five architects (and four structures) in the group of buildings, the Nordic countries were amply represented at Interbau in 1957. Arne Jacobsen, Kay Fisker, Alvar Aalo, Fritz Jaenecke, and Sten Samuelson all played a decisive role in the development of modern architecture in their respective countries. Nils-Ole Lund looks at a number of these architects in his essay (chapter 8 in the present anthology:

14 Hall: *Planning and Urban Growth in the Nordic Countries*, p. 258.

15 "A general interest in the Nordic welfare model certainly contributed to the attention these projects [e.g., Vällingby, CSH] aroused."Ibid.

16 "The prevailing opinion that social benefits can only be afforded with wealth is questionable. On the contrary: the European states are so rich because they grant such social benefits." Walter Rothholz: "Der skandinavische Wohlfahrtsstaat als Model für die Bundesrepublik?," in: Robert Bohn et al. (ed.): *Deutsch-skandinavische Beziehungen nach 1945*, Stuttgart: Franz Steiner Verlag, 2000, pp. 152-161, p. 159.

17 Rothholz: "Der skandinavische Wohlfahrtsstaat als Model für die Bundesrepublik?," p. 159.

"Going South. Danish and Nordic 'empiricism' and its representation at Interbau in 1957").[18]

Just how vulnerable the welfare state form of government was can be seen – with reference to the subject areas in the present anthology – most clearly in Finland, where enormous political pressure from the Soviets could only be resisted by a sophisticated balancing act by the government. The writings of the influential architect Alvar Aalto are a testament to such confrontations, as well as to national ideological exclusions and the fear of annexation. Finland's projected exemplary role clearly arises from a number of Aalto's publication titles, such as *Finland as a Model for World Development* (1949) or *Finland Wonderland* (1950). In a certain sense, Finland's geopolitical situation is comparable with Berlin's during the Cold War – and to that extent, the popularity of Aalto's contribution to Interbau may testify to his sensitive empathy for the neighborhood in divided Berlin. Eeva-Liisa Pelkonen discusses "Aalto and Finland's Geopolitical Dilemma" in chapter 5.

The position of Icelandic culture in the contemporary flash point of the Great Powers also illustrates both geopolitical vulnerability and the development of dedicated solutions. In chapter 7, "The Dream of Pure Form. Icelandic Reception of Modernist Thought and Architecture," Pétur Àrmansson shows how Icelandic architecture again shifted towards "Nordic modernism" after the Second World War.

In his article "'A Kind of Paradise and Role Model'? – North European Architecture and Urban Planning in German Programmatic Texts of the 1940s and 1950s," David Kuchenbuch explains the concept of societal and architectural order and in his discussion explores the question of how a societal and sociocultural harmonization of society was to be brought about via a reorganization of space (chapter 2). This endeavor was a fundamental element of the town planning discussion that preceded "Interbau in 1957." The new walls shone in the center of bomb-shattered Berlin, while the dream of a society or even community without ruptures seemed more remote than ever in the divided city.

In chapter 4, "The Structure of Desire in Architectural Modernism," Sven-Olov Wallenstein addresses the social climate and "esthetic mentality." His article aims to

18 See also Nils-Ole Lund: *Nordisk arkitektur*, Copenhagen: Politikens forlag, 2008.

trace the development process of modernism, which takes places on a pleasurable level and simultaneously belongs to a domain in which subconscious commitment and social instructions on how to act are linked, thus enabling a pleasure-driven esthetic perception in the field of tension between the individual and the collective. In this way, Wallenstein revises the topos of regulation or diktats of taste. His analysis also incorporates the political trends of modernism, which formed the foundations for the beginning of the Swedish "folkhem."

In her research, Ingeborg Glambeck investigates the reception of "Nordic Design" and architecture in the twentieth century. In the process, she develops a sensitivity to new contemporary trends and reactions to impulses from the North. Despite a fundamentally positive and appreciative response, striking differences are discernible in the definition of Nordic characteristics in an English or German context. Glambeck's monography, *Nordic Traits in Architecture and Design – As Seen by Others,*[19] deals more with impressions and perceptual patterns than concrete structures or buildings. In chapter 1 of this anthology, "'Nordic Form' as Seen from the Outside," Glambeck presents an overview of how the "Nordic" has been defined, i.e., which images and representations can be derived from these external perceptions.

In chapter 6, Mari Hvattum illustrates the changes to the low-rise high-density movement brought about by modernist architecture and exemplifies this with Norwegian residential construction in the 1950s (see "Modified Modernism: The Relational Architecture of the Low-Rise High-Density Movement").

In her discourse analysis of contemporary press criticism of Stockholm suburbs entitled "'Tear it down!' The Discourses of Suburban Criticism: What Are They Really Saying?" Lisbeth Söderqvist examines the expectations and implications criticism of the suburbs voices (see chapter 9). Within the scope of her analysis of opinions opposing modernist suburb architecture, she demonstrates the changing views of construction on Stockholm's periphery. At the foreground of her discussion is, on the one hand, modest Vällingby, and on the other the large-format "driver and shopping paradise" of Skärholmen, already attacked by journalists at its opening.

19 Ingeborg Glambek: *Det nordiske i arkitektur og design.*

A narrative, and with it a route, can also be established on the basis of the Nordic buildings of Interbau – demonstrated by the *stadtfinden_moderne* contribution to the Hansaviertel anniversary: a GPS-supported tour through the Hansaviertel.[20] With a combination of art and contemporary history, Matthias Ott/ Tido von Oppeln directed users in sound and image through the neighborhood with the help of their Palm computer route, called "Nordic Line," and thus also to the Nordic buildings. In chapter 10, "'... but it was based on an idea of mine!' Modern Art, Modernism and the Hansaviertel – Still Connected to the North," Matthias Ott presents the content of this project.

20 The technical equipment was made available on hire by the Academy of Arts on Hanseatenweg.

"NORDIC FORM" AS SEEN FROM THE OUTSIDE

THE INTERPRETATION OF NORDIC DESIGN AND ARCHITECTURE OUTSIDE THE REGION

Ingeborg Glambek

Some years ago, I participated in an inter-Scandinavian research project[1] on the so-called "Nordic" character in architecture and design in the twentieth century. The central question was whether this expression makes good sense. Is it correct that design and architecture from the Scandinavian or "Nordic" countries has a kind of common stamp or character? And if so, what are these common characteristics or features more precisely? And is it possible to give a relatively convincing definition?

My part of the project was to investigate how Nordic architecture and design were received and interpreted outside the Nordic region. It was a reception analysis based on articles, reviews, criticisms, reports, and surveys primarily in connection with Scandinavian representations at international exhibitions of architecture, crafts and design in the period from 1900 up to the 1950s. Main sources were periodicals, magazines, and journals of architecture and design, mostly in English and German. To a certain extent, I also consulted newspapers, books, and more general magazines.

The general impression was that Nordic, or Scandinavian, architecture and design have received much and mainly enthusiastic attention abroad. This success has certainly contributed to the international impression that there exists a particular Scandinavian-Nordic identity and culture.

Definitions of the Term "Nordic"

"The Nordic countries" and "the North" have in recent times mainly been associated with Scandinavian northern Europe. It was not always like that, however. Traditionally, the northern areas of both Germany and Holland were classified as belonging to the "Nordic countries."[2] In an even wider sense, the term "Nordic" included all European countries north of the Alps, in contrast to the Mediterranean countries. This purely topographical definition of "the Nordic" was more common in earlier

1 Under the auspices of *Joint Committee for Nordic Research Councils for the Humanities (NOS-H).*

2 This meaning occurs quite often in German and Dutch sources. An example is found in the writings of De-Stijl artist and writer Theo van Doesburg (1883-1931) who often wrote about "Nordic" culture. To him, this mostly meant just the Dutch and the German.

times, for instance in the renaissance. In present day English, we would tend to use the term "northern" in this connection. And likewise, today's German language distinguishes between "nordisch" and "nördlich." The term "Nordic" has also been used to designate Protestant, in contrast to Catholic, Europe. This use of the word is also misleading because many European countries situated far north are Catholic or Orthodox, for instance Russia and parts of the Baltic Countries. In recent times, the Baltic countries are often included in the term "Norden" or "the North" together with the three Scandinavian countries, Iceland, and Finland.

During the first decades of the twentieth century, the term "Nordic" was also frequently used in the infamous debate on human races. The term then designated certain characteristics, cultural expressions, and traditions claimed as being typical of a special branch of the Germanic race particularly common in Scandinavia, the so-called "Nordic-Germanic" race. In that period, it was also claimed that the Germanic, and in particular the Nordic-Germanic, race was superior to other human races. After World War Two, with its devastating consequences, however, extreme reservation has been applied in talking about human races at all. Consequently, after World War Two, it became very unpopular to use the term "Nordic" about cultural expressions as typical of a particular race as was done in the interwar period.

In the following, I will use the expressions "the North" and "the Nordic" in the way that is most common today, i.e., to refer, geographically and culturally, Scandinavian countries, Denmark, Norway and Sweden, to Finland, and to a certain extent Iceland (In the material from the period I have investigated however, from 1900 up to the 1960s, Iceland is hardly mentioned at all).

National versus Nordic Identity

Although the Scandinavians often feel they have a certain common Nordic identity, they also have clear notions of national characteristics. They primarily regard themselves as Danes, Finns, Icelanders, Norwegians, or Swedes and maintain there are characteristic differences between the particular countries in temperament, history, and culture. However, as is the case with the concept "Nordic," "national characteristics" are not easy to define. One is often left with stereotypes and clichés. We are all familiar with expressions like "jovial Danes," "stiff Swedes," "quiet Finns," "naïve Norwegians," but have problems trying to be more precise.[3]

Clichés are also common when talking more specifically about architecture and design. For instance, Swedish architects are often described as "rational, and conscious of material and function." Danish architecture and design is often characterized as being "simple and classic," Norwegian is "vigorous and expressive" and the Finnish style is "strong, conscious of form, close to nature and somewhat melancholy."[4] These characteristics are all quite abstract and not very precise. It turns out that it is equally difficult to be precise when talking about specific products. What is in fact meant by characterizing a building or a piece of furniture as typically "Nordic" or as having "an individual national stamp"?

In the following, I will discuss some concepts that were frequently used through the whole period from 1900 until well into the 1950s to describe Nordic architecture and design. These concepts are: "Modernity," "Tradition," "National characteristics," and "Nordic common features."

Modernity

Presumably the most dominant feature of the last Century up to circa 1970 was the enthusiasm for "the modern." The wish to appear modern pervaded all fields of society. The modern was seen as the key to a better and happier world. Enthusiasm for things modern was manifest even earlier, at least from the second half of the nineteenth century. The great international exhibitions of that century can be seen as a tribute to everything imbued with the concept of "the modern": progress, development, news, and change. This enthusiasm continued in the following century. Typical are the

3 The clichés are steadily in use. See for example the catalog to the inter-Scandinavian traveling exhibition Helena Dahlbäck Lutteman (ed.): *Nordisk form på 1990-talet: Nordic Design in the 1990s,* Stockholm: Nationalmuseum, 1994.

4 More details in Ingeborg Glambek: *Det nordiske i arkitektur og design sett utenfra,* Copenhagen: Arkitektens Forlag og Norsk arkitekturforlag, 1997.

programs and manifestos for the great, international exhibitions and fairs of the first half of the twentieth century. According to the invitations to participate in the Paris world fair of 1900, the purpose was to herald in the new century, to show how far the different nations had progressed within technology, science, and art and on this basis to sketch the future direction. The program for the first major international exhibition of decorative art and design, Torino 1902, emphasized that the aim was "to show artistic renewal" and specifically underlined that objects just "reproductions of existing styles"[5] would be rejected. It is significant that the terms "Art-Nouveau" (new art) and "Jugend" (youth) were coined in connection with these two exhibitions. Similar formulations can be found in the invitations, programs, and manifestos for other great exhibitions throughout the period.[6] As an example, the invitation to join the 1925 international exhibition in Paris stated that it was open to "all producers whose products are artistic and clearly show modern tendencies." And the official name of the 1937 world fair in Paris was "International Exhibition of Art and Technology in the Modern World."[7] The world Fair in New York two years later had as its motto: "The World of Tomorrow."

The organizers' ambitious aims of showing just modern and new artistic products were, however, far from realized. According to the majority of reviews and reports in professional periodicals for architecture and design, most of what was shown at these exhibitions and fairs was not modern at all. More often than not it was maintained that the products in art, architecture, and design were old-fashioned and nailed to traditions and clichés from former periods. The old "countries of culture" like England, France, Spain, and Italy, in particular, fell victim to this criticism. Products from these countries were, according to a majority of reviewers,[8] characterized as outdated,

5 Quoted in Elisabeth Gilmore Holt: *The Expanding World of Art 1874-1902,* New Haven and London: Yale University Press, 1988, p. 140.

6 On the international exhibitions and fairs in the nineteenth and twentieth centuries, see for instance: John Allwood: *The Great Exhibitions,* London: Studio Vista, 1977; Elisabeth G. Holt: *The Expanding World of Art;* Paul Greenhalgh: *Ephemeral Vistas. The Expositions Universelles, Great Exhibitions and World's Fairs 1851-1939,* Manchester: Manchester University Press, 1988; Peter B. MacKeith/ Kerstin Smeds: *The Finland pavilions: Finland at the Universal Expositions 1900-1992,* Tampere: Kustannus Oy City, 1993.

7 "Exposition Internationale des Arts et Techniques dans la Vie Moderne."

8 I have mainly concentrated on English and German language areas.

empty-phrased, formalistic, and constrained. The Nordic countries, however, were often mentioned as an exception to this sad and depressing situation. These countries attracted increasing attention at the international exhibitions of the early twentieth century. The architecture of their pavilions as well as the exhibited products were, according to the critics, seen as refreshingly new, "fresh winds from the North," as expressed by an Austrian critic. What was seen as the Nordic, fresh, original, and new was frequently polarized against the "outdated, dusty and worm-eaten." In nearly all reviews, the refrain was that the Nordic architects, artists, craftsmen, and designers, in contrast to exhibitors from southern countries, had managed to cross boundaries and create something new. When *The Studio* wrote in connection with the Paris exhibition 1900 that "in these remote countries a powerful art movement is facing its way into the general art development of Europe [...] [it] will undoubtedly ere [sic] long claim greater public attention"[9] and the German *Innendekoration* on the same occasion stated that the new century belonged to "the barbarians from the North,"[10] these were not isolated statements by isolated commentators, but examples of a widespread view.

Tradition

Tradition is another word that was widely used. This may appear paradoxical because it is difficult to see how tradition can be combined with modernity. But this was exactly what the critics and reviewers saw as specific to Nordic art, architecture, and design. In the Scandinavian countries, folkart and handicraft were still alive, it was claimed, and these were the sources that modern designers used for their inspiration. The reviewers maintained that roots in tradition combined with healthy public-mindedness *(Volkstümlichkeit)* and a democratic approach had resulted in a modern style that suited contemporary requirements and ways of life.[11] In connection with the Paris-exhibition of 1925, a Swiss periodical stated that the Nordic countries, to a

9 *The Studio,* no. 3, London, 1900, p. 199.

10 "Die nordischen Barbaren rücken vor [...] Ihnen werden die nächsten Jahrhunderte gehören." *Innendekoration,* Stuttgart/ Darmstadt: Koch, 1900, p. 106.

11 An example is *Kunst und Handwerk,* no. 7, München, 1904.

certain extent followed by Russia, Czechia, and Poland, had progressed towards a new, modern style. Sweden was particularly successful thanks to "exemplary co-operation between industry and artists and combined with a clearly traceable and unchanged tradition."[12]

The characterization of Nordic architecture and design as a form of modernism that was both popular *(volkstümlich)* – in the sense of warm and human – as well as simple and functional, and at the same time rooted in tradition, is repeatedly found in foreign reviews right up to the 1950s. The secret of the Scandinavians was, it was claimed, that they were inspired by rural and popular traditions without lapsing into copying and nostalgic use of isolated motifs, and that they managed to combine tradition with contemporary demands concerning appearance and function. In short, the Nordic language of form was seen as modern but not shockingly modern, and at the same time it was perceived as popular without being vulgar.

National Characteristics

Most reviewers took the common Nordic stamp in art, architecture and design as a matter of course without comment, as a kind of family-likeness. What was commonly seen as more interesting were the individual national characteristics and differences between the products from the individual countries. The strength in the artistic style of the different Scandinavian countries was, according to many commentators, that they were not trying to imitate each other. The Scandinavian or Nordic peoples were not aiming at being Nordic but respected each other's distinctive, national character, it was maintained. It is typical, wrote the German magazine *Kunst und Handwerk*, that the Swedes never try to be like Norwegians and, vice versa, that the Norwegians are not giving the impression they are Swedes.[13]

12 "[...] der vorzüglichen Zusammenarbeit ihrer Industrie mit den Künstlern und dank einer stark spürbaren, wenig alterierten Tradition." *Das Werk*, Bern, 1925, p. 185.

13 "[...] die Schweden niemals versuchen, Norweger zu sein, dass die Norweger niemals sich für Schweden ausspielen." *Kunst und Handwerk*, no. 1, München, 1900, p. 367.

The same year, the English Studio wrote: "Whatever likeness there may be between the northern peoples, the difference in character of the countries will always produce great contrasts in artistic styles."[14]

It is, however, not easy to catch the precise meaning of these references to special national qualities and characters. Presumably it is impossible to give precise definitions. The metaphor of family-resemblance *(Familienähnlichkeit)*[15] may be helpful here. It is usually possible to trace common features in members of a specific family, but there are always individual differences, no feature is common to all members of the same family, but usually there are a series of overlapping similarities. Consequently, it is difficult to describe more precisely the likenesses that define the family.

Statements about the national character in art and design products from the individual Scandinavian or Nordic countries were particularly common at the beginning of the twentieth century but less emphasized in the 1920s and 1930s, perhaps because this was the break-through period of "modernism" or functionalism in architecture and design, a period which was often simply called "the international style."[16] After World War Two, however, it was once more common to speak about different national "styles" in architecture and design.

Between 1954 and 1957, the Nordic countries collaborated on a big exhibition traveling the US and Canada presenting Scandinavian craft and design.[17] The Scandinavians wanted to present the results of a well-functioning collaboration between four different countries with different traditions and mentalities. The strategy was to "sell" Scandinavia with a common stamp and at the same time to underline the individual,

14 *The Studio,* no. 3, London, 1900, p. 196.

15 The philosopher Ludwig Wittgenstein (1889-1951) is famous for his use of this concept.

16 Named after the title of a book written by Henry Russell Hitchcock and Philip Johnson to follow an exhibition on architecture curated by them at the Museum of Modern Art in New York in 1932. The exhibition showed buildings of the day in fifteen countries. Represented were, among others, Le Corbusier, Oud, Gropius, van der Rohe, Alto, Markelius, Åhren. Henry-Russell Hitchcock and Philip Johnson: *The International Style,* New York: Norton, 1995.

17 The exhibition, *Design in Scandinavia* (1954-57), was initiated by Elizabeth Gordon, editor of the American magazine *House Beautiful,* and realized in co-operation with American Federation of Arts.

national differences.[18] The slogan "Scandinavian Design" was coined in connection with this exhibition and judging from the many descriptions, reports, and reviews, the individual, national characteristics in the exhibits were conspicuous.

When reading the reviews more closely, one is struck by the similarity of their formations. Often, the wordings are taken directly from invitations, programs, and catalogs presenting the exhibition. The impression is that the authors of reviews and articles have been briefed by the organizers. One suspects that the reporters and reviewers, as well as the general public, would probably not have noticed the individual national characteristics of the exhibits if they had not been so emphatically made aware of them. The conception of a Scandinavian/Nordic common stamp in combination with clear individual/national characteristics was obviously the result of a conscious policy of the people in charge. This turned out to be a most successful marketing strategy. "Scandinavian Design" proved a very effective slogan. It simultaneously promoted sales, satisfied national needs for assertion, and met international demands for something special, new and moderately exotic.

Nordic Modernity and Social-Democratic Values

Architecture, design, and crafts from the Nordic or Scandinavian countries evidently appeared as having a special character, but it is not easy to sort out more exactly what their common stamp consisted in. As mentioned, the descriptions were mostly given in general and imprecise terms. Sometimes, particularly in the first part of the investigated period, "heavy ornamentation" was mentioned as typically Nordic, sometimes the "simple, straight, clean, and classical." Nevertheless, judging from both English and German sources through the period from the turn of the century up to 1950s, it is obvious that there is "something" that is conceived as typically Nordic. However, what was seen as typical Nordic characteristics was also closely linked to more general preferences, trends, and styles of the period. The great international

18 The term "sell" can also be taken literally. As the traveling exhibition was shown in museums, department stores and shops along the route presented heavily advertised exhibitions showing Scandinavian design products for sale. This sales promotion proved very successful.

exhibition of architecture and design in Stockholm in 1930 under the auspices of Swedish Society of Craft and Industrial Design (Svenska Slöjdföreningen),[19] demonstrated that Sweden, and to a certain extent all of Scandinavia, had assimilated and further developed ideas that originally were promoted elsewhere, particularly in Central Europe, Germany, and Holland. Keywords here are "Deutscher Werkbund" (German Association of Architects, Designers, and Industrialists), "Bauhaus," and "Wohnung für das Existenzminimum" (Dwellings for lower income groups). The Nordic modern interacted with the international modernism promoted by liberal and left wing politics. Catchwords and phrases originally stamped by Swedish design pioneers like "Beauty for everybody" (Skönhet åt alla) and "Better things for everyday life" (Vackrara vardagsvara) came into general use.[20]

The English were particularly enthusiastic about what they saw as the Scandinavian-Nordic way of life. Scandinavia was seen as an example of successful social planning. In these countries, important social-democratic values like simplicity, social equality, and justice had to a great degree been realized. It was constantly repeated that the Scandinavian countries were among the most progressive and well-organized in Europe.[21] Sweden has a very high architectural standard, wrote the *RIBA Journal*, maybe the most prestigious English architectural periodical, in 1939, and the reason is that the country is without "extremes of wealth and poverty."[22] Swedish architecture is an architecture for the people, it is an architecture of "an informed and cultural democracy." Coming back from a study tour in Sweden, a correspondent in another English periodical wrote that it had been the greatest experience of his life. "It was my first and only experience of civilization."[23] He maintains that Sweden is a country of complete harmony and balance thanks to its social system. In this country, culture and "good taste" is not something reserved for a particular class, but belongs to the people.

19 From 1976 it was called "Svensk Form."

20 "Skönhet åt alla" is a catchword launched by author and social reformer Ellen Key (1849-1926). "Vackrare vardagsvara" originally title of book (issued 1919) by Gregor Paulsson, art historian and first director of Svenska Slöjdföreningen.

21 An example is *Architectural Association Journal*, London, 1939, p. 217.

22 *RIBA Journal*, no. 1, London, January 1939.

23 *Architectural Design and Construction*, November 1938, p. 420.

"Civilized" was an adjective often used in connection with Sweden and the Swedish. For instance, in his well-known book *Sweden Builds*, G.E. Kidder Smith writes: "The one adjective appropriate to describe Swedish architecture … is CIVILIZED" [sic].[24] Like many others, Kidder Smith regarded Nordic modernism as the architectural style of social democracy: "It is difficult to imagine their architecture in a non-socialist country."[25]

Nordic modernism culminated in the Scandinavian Design period of the 1950s and 1960s. From the end of 1960s, however, the optimistic belief in development and progress was undermined by well-aimed criticism and ironic attacks by the movement called post-modernism. At this time, the Scandinavian social model was also beginning to crumble as an international ideal. This was partly because the ideas of the welfare state had in large measure been realized and therefore were less challenging, partly because these ideas now were seen as moralistic, rigid, and authoritarian, and partly because the system was becoming too expensive to sustain. Many of the values cherished by social democracy and Nordic architecture and design from the breakthrough in the 1930s, "beautiful everyday products," "good and healthy housing for everyone," etc., gradually appeared as quite banal, somewhat naïve and – worst of all – "normative" and moralistic. Such norms are not viable in a world where the diversity, individualism, and pluralism of values take the place of honor.

About the author

Ingeborg Glambek, Ph.D., is professor of art history at the University of Oslo. Her main field is architecture and design history, and she has published various books and articles on these subjects. Glambek's interest in teaching art history resulted in the publication of her popular scholarly book on general art history: *Om Kunst de siste 200 år.* (1994). Her book *Det nordiske i arkitektur og design sett utefra* (1997) covered the reception of Nordic traits in architecture and design as seen by others, and her latest book, *Selvportret. En kunsthistorie* (2008), offers a view on the history of self portraits through time.

24 George Everard Kidder Smith: *Sweden Builds*, London: Architectural Press, 1957 [1950], p. 18. Contemporary reviews of Kidder-Smith's book regarded him as somewhat too enthusiastic and simplified, for instance *The Architectural Review. A Magazine of Architecture and Decoration*, no. 1, London, 1952, p. 55.

25 Kidder Smith: *Sweden Builds*, 1957, p. 18.

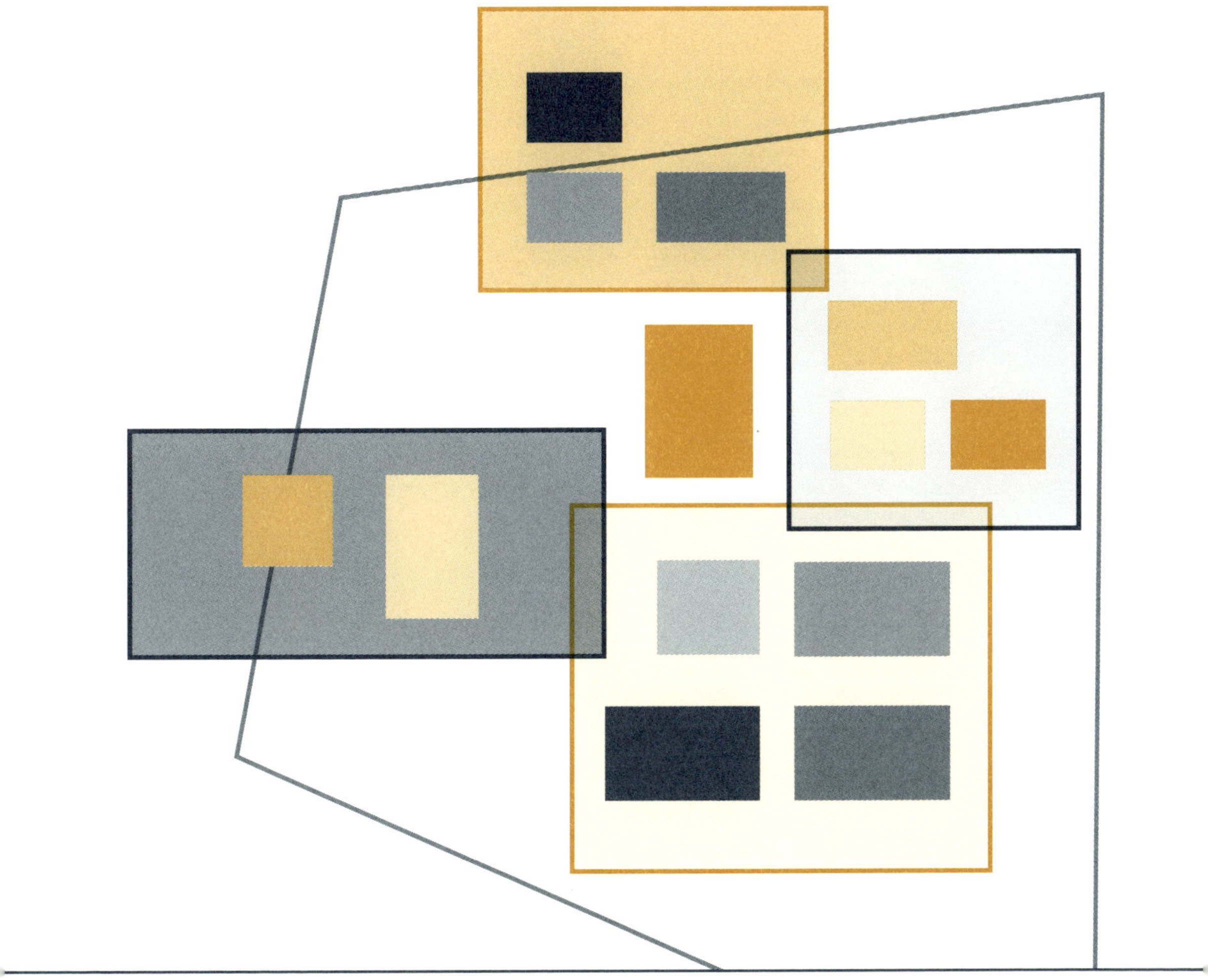

A KIND OF PARADISE AND ROLE MODEL?

NORTH EUROPEAN ARCHITECTURE AND URBAN PLANNING IN GERMAN PROGRAMMATIC TEXTS OF THE 1940s AND 1950s

David Kuchenbuch

Anyone who studies German architecture of the 1950s will sooner or later be confronted with the claim that it was influenced by the "humanity" or "humaneness" of North European modernism. It is not clearly defined what this humanity, this moderation, or modest character, consists of. At times we get the impression that the use of certain materials, wood and brick in particular, is decisive; sometimes a sense of detail or the balanced dimensions of settlements are mentioned; and often the importance of welfare architecture – good schools, public housing – is highlighted. Obviously, this is a cliché: that of a North European humility and modernity, of the Scandinavian ideal of consensus.[1] But let us examine three statements on the "Nordic influence" more closely. On the one hand, Kenneth Frampton's canonical *Modern Architecture* portrays the monumentalism of 1950s' English Brutalism as a reaction to what was known in Great Britain as *people's detailing or new empiricism* – a modest, supposedly Nordic welfare architecture – and as an attempt to form a link with the 1920s.[2] In the current Hamburg architecture guide on the other hand, Dirk Meyhöfer discusses the Hamburg residential area *Groß Borstel,* planned by Werner Kallmorgen in the mid-1950s, in contrast to the neighboring area, *Klein Borstel,* which was built during the Third Reich. The former, Meyhöfer says, possesses a "different ideological orientation," because here the "imaginary Scandinavian model is involved."[3] In both

1 See Kazimierz Musial: *Tracing the Roots of the Scandinavian Model. Image of Progress in the Era of Modernisation,* Florence/Berlin: European University Institute, 1998. Just how deeply-rooted this stereotype is can been seen in a text for a guided tour of buildings by North European architects in the Hansaviertel in Berlin, found on the tour office's website: "In the Nordic line, the Scandinavian countries are grouped together as a collective metaphor for 'modern societies'" (http://www.stadtfinden-moderne.de/ [last accessed: 7.04.2008]). The Nordic and modernism are congruent here, the North European contributions represent the model for the exhibition as a whole.

2 Surprisingly, in this heavily canonized book Northern Europe is only represented by Alvar Aalto and Gunnar Asplund in his neoclassical phase. Cf. Kenneth Frampton: *Modern Architecture: A Critical History,* London: Thames and Hudson, 2007. On *new empiricism* see e.g.: Eva Rudberg: "Vardagens utopi. Svenskt och osvenskt i funktionalismens arkitektur," in: Cecilia Widenheim and Eva Rudberg (eds.): *Utopi och verklighet. Svensk modernism 1900-1960. Moderna Museet 7 oktober - 14 januari 2001,* Stockholm: Norstedts, 2001, pp. 150-173; a more critical approach is found in Kenneth Frampton: "Stockholm 1930. Asplund and the legacy of funkis," in: Claes Caldenby Claes and Olof Hultin (eds.): *Asplund,* Stockholm: Arkitektur Förlaget, 1985, pp. 35-39.

3 Dirk Meyhöfer: *Hamburg. Der Architekturführer,* Hamburg/Berlin: Braun, 2007, p. 153. Some pages before it is said of a school built by Gerhard Laage that a "human, 'Danish' standard" influenced the building (ibid., p. 150). According to Cornehl, it was above all *Gustavsberg* near Stockholm that served as a model for Groß Borstel. Ulrich Cornehl: *"Raummassagen."* Der Architekt Werner Kallmorgen 1902-1979, Hamburg: Dölling und Galitz, 2003, p. 97, footnote 439.

cases, Nordic architecture is contrasted with more radical architectural phenomena. Here, Northern architecture – the brickwork houses, the practical, yet occasionally eclectically ornamented buildings à la Sven Backström and Leif Reinius – is presented as an aesthetic *third way*. It is situated somewhere between *Neues Bauen* (typically characterized by white plaster and transparency, symbols of "liberated living,"[4] or a "place-dissolving," "serial settlement texture"[5]) and the limestone fantasies of the Fascistic "word of stone."[6] But there are even more interpretations: Winfried Nerdinger, for example, considers the modernist "griditis," which was particularly prevalent in Germany the 1950s, to be heavily influenced by Nordic style. He explains this as the result of a desire of German postwar architecture to distance itself from National Socialism.[7] However, Nerdinger also shows that the fascination for the rationality represented by the grid was already widespread during the "Third Reich."[8] Moreover, he concedes that in the Germany of the 1930s and 1940s there was a strong North European influence – in particular due to Steen Eiler Rasmussen's *Nordische Baukunst* (Nordic architecture) of 1940 and articles in *Moderne Bauformen.*[9]

---

4 Andreas K. Vetter: *Die Befreiung des Wohnens. Ein Architekturphänomen der 20er und 30er Jahre,* Tübingen: Wasmuth, 2000.

5 Michael Peterek: *Wohnung. Siedlung. Stadt. Paradigmen der Moderne 1910-1950,* Berlin: Mann, 2000, pp. 147ff.

6 To English planners, says Eric Mumford, Swedish architecture appeared to be the "middle way between Stalinist socialist realism and the 'tougher' kinds of modernism soon to be exemplified by [Le Corbusier's] Unité." Eric Mumford: *The CIAM Discourse on Urbanism, 1928-1960,* Cambridge, Mass.: MIT Press, 2000, p. 167.

7 Winfried Nerdinger: "Materialästhetik und Rasterbauweise. Zum Charakter der Architektur der 50er Jahre," in: Werner Durth and Niels Gutschow: *Architektur und Städtebau der fünfziger Jahre. Ergebnisse der Fachtagung in Hannover 1990.* Bonn: Deutsches Nationalkomitee für Denkmalschutz, 1998, pp. 38-49, p. 42, 47.

8 This is apparent with Ernst Neufert, who had been on Gropius' staff in the early 1930s and who in the 1940s was commissioner for the standardization of industrial architecture under Albert Speer. On Neufert: Walter Prigge (ed.): *Ernst Neufert. Normierte Baukultur im 20. Jahrhundert,* Dessau/ Frankfurt a.M.: Campus Verlag, 1999. Neufert made trips to Scandinavia during the 1930s. Cf. Ernst Neufert: "Bauen und Bauten bei unseren nordischen Nachbarn," in: *Monatshefte für Baukunst und Städtebau* no. 17, 1933, pp. 545-552.

9 Incidentally, in Rasmussen's book the vilified signals of modernism turn up: platform roof, large windows, seriality, etc. Here we find photos of *Stockholmsutställningen* in 1930 and of the modernistic Copenhagen apartment buildings in *Storgården and Klokkergården.* Cf. Steen Eiler Rasmussen: *Nordische Baukunst. Beispiele und Gedanken zur Baukunst unserer Zeit in Dänemark und Schweden,* Berlin: Wasmuth, 1940, pp. 158-163, pp. 164ff. In a eulogy to Arne Jacobsen in 1940, Werner Kallmorgen said: "It is only thanks to Steen Eiler Rasmussen's book on 'Nordic Architecture' that we learned that one must go to Gothenburg." Quoted after Cornehl: *Raummassagen,* p. 66.

The thesis implicit in all three statements, namely that the importance of Scandinavian architecture as a role model, stemmed from its (more or less) restrained modernist character and its democratic ambitions, is of no real help: the connection between politics and design remains vague.

It is evident that architecture and urban planning in the Nordic countries made a great impression on German architects in the wake of the destruction of German cities during World War Two. Friedrich Spengelin stated that the buildings in 1950s Sweden were a "Mecca" for his generation of planners;[10] following his visit there in 1950, Hubert Hoffmann regarded Sweden as "a kind of paradise and role-model";[11] Carl Bauer remembers that "the Swedish impressions of that time, especially social housing, were like a dream";[12] Konstanty Gutschow traveled to Sweden in 1951 and thenceforth began corresponding with Swedish architects in order to furnish his textbook *Städtebaulicher Grundstoff* with examples.[13]

However, when one inquires what the main themes were in the reciprocal reception between Swedish and German architects before 1945, one is confronted with an interesting phenomenon: although the Swedish functionalists expressed their abhorrence at the undemocratic (and above all non-functional) National Socialist aesthetic,[14] they absorbed many German studies of a mere technical character, which in turn were compatible with National Socialist ideology.[15] After a phase of traditionalist *völkisch*

10 Hans Kampfmeyer et al.: "Zu Beginn der 60er Jahre hatten wir das Gefühl: Jetzt müssen wir von Grund auf neu anfangen," in: *Stadtbauwelt*, no. 88, 1985, pp. 326-337, p. 332. Kähler also emphasized that *Vällingby* was the "Mecca of socially responsible modern urbanism," Gerd Kähler: "Reisen bildet. Der Blick nach Außen," in: Ingeborg Flagge (ed.): *Geschichte des Wohnens. Vol. 5. 1945 bis heute. Aufbau, Neubau, Umbau*, Stuttgart: Deutsche Verlagsanstalt, 1999, pp. 949-1036, p. 955. See also the travel journal of a group of architects from Hamburg: Arthur Dähn (ed.): *Eine Reise durch Süd-Schweden*. 27.5.-6.6.1953, Hamburg: Hammonia Verlag, 1953.

11 Hubert Hoffmann: "Eine Art Paradies und Vorbild 1950: Schweden," *Akademie der Künste Berlin, Baukunstarchiv* (ADK), Hubert Hoffmann, HHof 65.

12 Quoted after Durth and Gutschow (eds.): *Architektur und Städtebau der fünfziger Jahre*, 103.

13 "Reise nach Schweden. 2.-13.10.1951," *Staatsarchiv Hamburg*, StA-HH, 621 - 2/11 Bauarchiv Konstanty Gutschow, C 81.

14 See e.g., Gunnar Sundbärg: "Fackmännens neutralitet," in: *Byggmästaren*, vol. 12, no. 20, 1933, pp. 23-25.

15 Dirk Schubert: "Gottfried Feder und sein Beitrag zur Stadtplanungstheorie – technokratische Richtwertplanung oder nationalsozialistische Stadtplanungsideologie?" in: *Die alte Stadt*, no. 13, 1986, pp. 193-211.

architecture after 1933, in the late 1930s scientific planning of residential space was re-evaluated in Germany – mostly due to arms manufacture and increased industrial production, which required mass housing. This was closely observed by Swedish architects: Jöran Curman's *Industrins arbetarebostäder* (industrial workers settlements) of 1944 made reference to Neufert's *Bauentwurfslehre* (building design practice) and *Die neue Stadt* (the new city) by Gottfried Feder – the latter was the leading ideologue of the "socialist" wing of the Nazi Party for some years.[16] Feder's study was considered by some planners as a breakthrough in the search for a "Swedish Mumford."[17] And in a collection of standards that was of central importance for the financing of residential building – the *Westholmbibeln* - the *Richtlinien zur Verordnung zum zukünftigen Wohnungsbau* (guidelines for the regulation of future construction of residential building) of 15 November 1940 were referenced[18] – the commencement of "Fordist" social housing construction under the leadership of the DAF (the German Labour Front) in Germany.[19] In a 1950 review of Sweden in the 1940s, Yngve Larsson went as far as to state the following:

> One can certainly find – though few like to admit it nowadays – traces of ideological influences from the south. These influences were not only a result of the admiration for the impressive technocratic planned economy with its vast proportions, also in the field of urban planning, of highways and the prestigious boulevards as a symbol of the Thousand-year Reich, but equally by the particular illusionary democracy of the dictatorship, which, with its mass

16 Jöran Curman: *Industrins arbetarebostäder,* Uppsala: Industriens utredninsinstitut, 1944, 157, 130. During a conference in 1940, Feder, on the other hand, described his impressions of the congress of the *Internationalen Verbandes für Wohnungswesen und Städtebau* in Stockholm 1939: "Deutsche Akademie für Städtebau, Reichs- und Landesplanung. Jahresversammlung der Deutschen Akademie für Städtebau, Reichs- und Landsplanung," in: *Raumordnung und Raumforschung,* vol. 4, 1940, pp. 132-134.

17 Bertil Hök: "En svensk 'Mumford,'" in: *Byggmästaren,* vol. 22, 1943, pp. 34-35.

18 Sigurd Westholm: *Minimifordringar å storleken av bostadslägenheter i hus avsedda att uppföras med stöd av staligt tertiärlån,* Stockholm: Meddelanden från Statens byggnadslånebyrå, 1942, p. 15.

19 See Gerhard Fehl: "Welcher Fordismus eigentlich?" in: Regina Bittner et al. (eds.): *Zukunft aus Amerika. Fordismus in der Zwischenkriegszeit,* Frankfurt a.M./ New York: Dessau: Stiftung Bauhaus Dessau und Rheinisch-Westfälische Technische Hochschule Aachen, 1995, pp. 32ff.

rallies at sports festivals, not to mention *Kraft durch Freude* (Strength through Joy), also had a suggestive effect on neutral bystanders...[20] [My translation. Italics are German in the original text]

The degree of innovation and "modernity" in German post-war architecture should not be judged on a purely aesthetic level – there was no re-import of modern architecture from the North. The recourse to an aesthetic reassessment following the Nordic example is possibly a relic of a rationale that aimed at identifying the neoclassical architecture in the Nazi era (as well as in the GDR) as a dictatorial style *per se*. This is a justification which Gerhard Fehl has opposed with the thesis of the "programmatic eclecticism"[21] in National Socialist architecture. It was also refuted in the 1980s in a series of studies on the continuity of Bauhaus architecture beyond 1933. Of course, after 1945 many architects had great interest in introducing a kind of "zero hour" on a stylistic level. However, it is easy to overlook the fact that this did not necessarily concern concepts that were felt to be dictated by "practical constraints" of a technical but also of a sociological nature and that had been discussed within a transnational context before 1945. The focus on *stylistic* modernity can result in blindness for continuities in urbanism.

I would like to propose that we have to see the reception of North European architectural and urban planning concepts by German planners in the context of a transnational style of thought:[22] German planners projected an *Ordnungsdenken* – an ideology of Order – on the North. I will subsequently attempt to prove this by taking a look at how Northern Europe appears in a series of publications in the discourse around the Interbau exhibition in Berlin 1957. I will analyze texts by Hans Bernhard Reichow, Johannes Göderitz, Roland Rainer, and Hubert Hoffmann in order to characterize their manner of assessing North European architecture and urban planning.

20 Yngve Larsson: "1940-talets stadsbyggnadskonst. Några lekmannabetraktelser," in: *Plan*, vol. 1, 1950, pp. 5-11, p. 5.

21 Gerhard Fehl: *Kleinstadt, Steildach, Volksgemeinschaft. Zum "reaktionären Modernismus" in Bau- und Stadtbaukunst*, Braunschweig et al.: Vieweg, 1995, p. 180.

22 On the notion of "style of thought" or "thought-style" cf. Ludwig Fleck: *Entstehung und Entwicklung einer wissenschaftlichen Tatsache. Einführung in die Lehre vom Denkstil und Denkkollektiv.* Mit einer Einleitung hg. von Lothar Schäfer und Thomas Schnelle, Frankfurt a.M.: Suhrkamp, 1980 [1935].

Firstly, however, we need to characterize Ordnungsdenken. Its lowest common denominator was the moral conviction that experts had to serve the common good. Thus, architects set off to fight the "social issues" of the "liberal epoch" – the socially-fragmented nineteenth century. Its problems – "chaotic," health-threatening urbanization, "massification," class antagonisms, etc. – seemed to architects to be solvable through rational budgeting with economic and demographic resources. For architects and urban planners, the social community was in crisis. Therefore, space planned according to the "human scale" was intended to re-establish a relationship between the individual and the collective. Spatial structures that would form communities were advocated – neighborhood units, community centres, collective houses. These had to be based on preconceived social categories (*Ordnungen* in German) such as "family," "group," and "neighborhood."[23] This, planners said, would even lead to greater productivity. Everywhere in Europe, the intertwining of a crisis postulate and planning optimism led to apparently paradoxical reactions to modernity: technical and scientific modernization processes were connected to utopian but also pre- and even anti-modern objectives.[24] There was an overlap between a conservative Ordnungsdenken and a future-oriented social engineering.[25] Typical of this discourse is the reference to biological categories such as the body, health, and nature, categories that were thought to be stable beyond time and politics.

I would like to begin with Hans Bernhard Reichow's books *Organische Stadtbaukunst* (organic urban architecture) of 1948 and *Organische Baukunst* (organic architecture) of 1949. These were two of the first postwar publications on architecture and urban

23 See Lutz Raphael: "Sozialexperten in Deutschland zwischen konservativem Ordnungsdenken und rassistischer Utopie (1918-1945)," in: Wolfgang Hardtwig (ed.): *Utopie und politische Herrschaft*, München: Oldenbourg, 2003, pp. 327-346.

24 See Jeffrey Herf: *Reactionary Modernism. Technology, Culture, and Politics in Weimar and the Third Reich*, Cambridge, Mass.: Cambridge University Press, 1984.

25 See Thomas Etzemüller: "Die Romantik des Reißbretts. Social Engineering und demokratische Volksgemeinschaft in Schweden: Das Beispiel Alva und Gunnar Myrdal (1930-1960)," in: *Geschichte und Gesellschaft* 32, 2006, pp. 445-466; Zygmunt Bauman: *Dialektik der Ordnung. Die Moderne und der Holocaust*, Hamburg: Europäische Verlagsanstalt, 1992.

planning in Germany, which incidentally were reviewed in Sweden as "stimulating."[26] They prove to be a cornucopia of North European examples.[27] Reichow shows, for example, floor plans in *Kvarnholmen* and the "floor plan of a rooming house in Stockholm" (Markelius' Collective House in Stockholm). He describes the traffic routing of the *Slussen* in Stockholm as "a not inelegant solution [...] on an engineering and aesthetic level" and enthusiastically discusses the "split routing of the cycle paths in Copenhagen."[28] Reichow presents the Henningsen House near Copenhagen and Aalto's competition design for the "Town Hall in Nynäshamn" and advocates the airport in Bromma in Stockholm as a "universal symbol for all organic design." He expresses pleasure in the University of Aarhus by Kay Fisker, P. Stegmann, and C.F. Møller; discusses the star-shaped houses by Backström and Reinius in Gröndal; and praises the "organic design" of buildings by Alvar Aalto and Albin Stark in Nynäshamn as well as the "standard Swedish kitchen of the HSB."[29] Reichow mentions Gunnar Asplund, Gunnar Forszén, Rolf Engströmer, N.E. Eriksson, Helge Zimdal and Nils Ahrbom, Nils Koppel, G.N. Brandt and many others. A list of the illustrations in Reichow's book shows forty-nine examples from Northern Europe. The USA takes only second place with seventeen examples. In the *Organische Stadtbaukunst* we find the site plan of the *Aluminium City* by Walter Gropius and Marcel Breuer, which inspired the original, anti-axial design by Gerhard Jobst and Willy Kreuer for the Interbau, the Hansaviertel in Berlin.[30] It is interesting to note that Reichow placed this illustration next to the site plan of *Danviksklippan* in Stockholm.[31] This to be interpreted in connection with Reichow's almost defiant claim:

26 Hans Bernhard Reichow: *Organische Stadtbaukunst.* Von der Großstadt zur Stadtlandschaft, Braunschweig: Westermann, 1948. Hans Bernhard Reichow: *Organische Baukunst,* Braunschweig: Westermann, 1949. The review can be found in *Plan,* vol. 3/4, 1949.

27 Reichow's library contains a large collection of material on Swedish architecture. See "Schweden," *Germanisches Nationalmuseum Nürnberg, Archiv für bildende Kunst* (GNMN), Reichow, Hans Bernhard, I B 284 sqq. Reichow also visited Vällingby in 1957.

28 Reichow: *Organische Stadtbaukunst,* p. 103, 116.

29 Reichow: *Organische Baukunst,* p. 24, 40, 57, 50 sqq.

30 Cf. Gabi Dolff-Bonekämper: *Das Hansaviertel: Internationale Nachkriegsmoderne in Berlin,* Berlin: Verlag für Bauwesen, 1999, p. 19.

31 Reichow: *Organische Baukunst,* p. 48.

> The ideas in this book were conceived in their basic form before the destruction of many our cities had begun during the devastating war. Thus they demand, independent of these historical events, attention for the reorganization and recovery of all urban life and for the design of its visible expression.[32]

In Reichow's books, North European architecture emerges in an orchestration of feasibility, which, in view of the rather pragmatic reconstruction activities in post-war Germany, possesses a utopian character. Reichow's organicisms combine natural mysticism, biological needs, and nature as a model of efficient energy usage – his concept of a "branched" road system is infamous. Moreover, "organic design" implies, in functional terms, "the complete compatibility and congruity of the outward appearance with the inner content."[33] But most importantly, the adjective "organic" is used by Reichow to describe social harmony within the "urban landscape." It naturalizes community life within rationally-organized residential environments. Reichow propagates the neighborhood unit that was developed by Clarence Perry in the 1920s. But as he implicitly admits, this planning concept was also endorsed in the Third Reich where the Nazi *Ortsgruppe*, the local group of the NSDAP, was interpreted as "settlement cell" by Reichow, Gutschow, Göderitz, and others.[34] The idea of a small, manageable living environment that transcended social class was equally tempting to the apologists of the *Volksgemeinschaft* as to advocates of the American community spirit such as Perry.[35] Reichow regarded Sweden as a proof for the validity of such concepts.[36]

32 Ibid., p. VII.

33 Ibid., p. 74.

34 See Elke Pahl-Weber: "Die Ortsgruppe als Siedlungszelle," in: Michael Bose et al. (eds.): "… *Ein neues Hamburg entsteht …" Planen und Bauen von 1933-1945,* Hamburg: VISA-Verlag, 1986, pp. 46-55.

35 See Dirk Schubert: "'Heil aus Ziegelstein' - Aufstieg und Fall der Nachbarschaftsidee. Eine deutsch-anglo-amerikanische Dreiecks-Planungsgeschichte," in: *Die alte Stadt,* no. 25, 1998, pp. 141-173.

36 Reichow: *Organische Baukunst,* p. 17. This also becomes clear when he repeatedly compares his later plans for Sennestadt near Bielefeld with Vällingby in Stockholm. Cf. Reichow, Hans Bernhard: "Das Ende des hippodamischen Städtebaus," in: *Baukunst und Werkform,* vol. 8, 1955, pp. 532-553.

Another important text in the postwar architecture debate, Roland Rainer's 1948 *Die Behausungsfrage* (The Dwelling Question), a plea for the single-family house based on demographical considerations, on which Rainer had already worked before 1945 in the *Deutsche Akademie für Städtebau, Reichs- und Landesplanung*, is filled with examples from Northern Europe, many of which stem from Rasmussen's monograph.[37] And even the most important urban planning text of the 1950s does not fail to make reference to the North: *Die gegliederte und aufgelockerte Stadt* (The Segmented and Loosely-Structured City) by Johannes Göderitz, Roland Rainer, and Hubert Hoffmann of 1957, which also was a product of the *Deutsche Akademie* of the early 1940s.[38] In this text, "Gesundung" (recuperation) on every level is the objective. The social body can be healed if the integration and the productivity of its cells are enhanced by planning. Rejected forms of housing are "deformities and symptoms of degeneracy"; "if it [the body of the city] is completely healthy, the people living in it and forming it will be of healthy mind too."[39] The book starts with a quote by Fred Forbat, who was planning in Sweden:

> Every visitor from abroad who, when viewing our new residential areas, is enchanted and appalled by the diversity of the newly-constructed high-rise blocks, is compelled to ask me why Sweden builds high-rise residential blocks.[40]

The visitor's perspective on Sweden introduces a study that suggests an identity of democratic and authoritarian planning ideas: it references Lewis Mumford and Le Corbusier, *Harlow New Town* and German "settlement cell" concepts. The authors also illustrate their plea for a small scale "urban landscape" with graphic material from the

37 Roland Rainer: *Die Behausungsfrage,* Wien: Gallus-Verlag, 1947.

38 Johannes Göderitz et al.: *Die gegliederte und aufgelockerte Stadt,* Tübingen: Wasmuth, 1957.

39 Ibid., pp. 90-92.

40 Ibid., introduction to chapter VII, n. pag.

Interbau exhibition, Die Stadt von Morgen (The City of Tomorrow).[41] We see the site plan of a "city unit for approximately 10,000 inhabitants in central Sweden" by Fred Forbat. (In fact, as can be read in Fred Forbat's memoirs, the planners Karl Otto and Erich Kühn had approached Forbat in order to provide the exhibition with an example of Swedish planning.[42] Forbat, CIAM member, former assistant of Gropius and colleague of Ernst May, had emigrated to Sweden in 1939 on the initiative of Uno Åhréns. Forbat claims to have influenced the methods of plan layout and model design on the exhibition.[43]) Besides texts from the *Reichsforschungsgesellschaft für Wirtschaftlichkeit im Bau- und Wohnungswesen* (RFG), which place the book in a continuum with the Neues Bauen of the Weimar period, the *Gegliederte und aufgelockerte Stadt* lists the publication *Medizin und Städtebau* (Medicine and City Planning) as a reference.[44] This two-volume book can, according to editor Erich Kühn, be considered a result of the collaboration of "specialists, women's associations, sociologists, doctors, etc." in the preparatory committee of the exhibition Die Stadt von Morgen. It was published just in time for the Interbau.[45] In their book, Kühn and Heinrich Vogler brought together architects who had Third Reich entanglements such as Gutschow, "internal

41 See also Karl Otto: *die stadt von morgen. gegenwartsprobleme für alle,* Berlin: Mann, 1959. This text seems like a supplement to the *Gegliederte und aufgelockerte Stadt.* This becomes clear when a discussion of Hubert Hoffmann's site plan for Moabit in *Baukunst und Werkform* is augmented by quotes from *Die gegliederte und aufgelockerte Stadt*: Cf. Hoffmann, Hubert: "Eine Wohneinheit für 10 000 Einwohner, Berlin Moabit," in: *Baukunst und Werkform,* vol. 11, 1958, pp. 96-98. On the exhibition see Sandra Wagner-Conzelmann: *Die Interbau in 1957 in Berlin. Stadt von heute – Stadt von morgen. Städtebau und Gesellschaftskritik der 50er Jahre,* Petersberg: Imhof, 2007; Anette Maechtel and Kathrin Peters (eds.): *die stadt von morgen. beiträge zu einer archäologie des hansaviertels berlin,* Köln: König, 2008.

42 Fred Forbat's memoirs are a good source on the contact between German and Swedish architects in the 1950s. A copy can be found in the *Bauhausarchiv Berlin* (BAB), Fred Forbat: "Erinnerungen eines Architekten aus vier Ländern." Manuskripte 8. Fünf Jahre in Ungarn, 9. In Schweden. 1969-1972, Mappe 5, p. 276.

43 Ibid., 277. Forbat contributed significantly to the formation of a German CIAM group. See also the correspondence between Hoffmann and Forbat: "Korrespondens CIAM." 1951-1953, *Arkitekturmuseets Arkiv, Stockholm* (AAS), Fred Forbat, AM 1970-18-156, K 15. In the 1950s, Forbat frequently reported on regional planning in Sweden for the German magazine *Raumforschung und Raumordnung.*

44 Paul Vogler and Erich Kühn (eds.): *Medizin und Städtebau. Ein Handbuch für den gesundheitlichen Städtebau,* München/ Berlin/ Wien: Urban und Schwarzenberg, 1957, pp. 634-651.

45 Erich Kühn: "Die Fünfziger Jahre. Persönliche Erinnerungen an die Zeit des Wiederaufbaus," in: *Arch+* 56, 1981, pp. 22-27, p. 26.

exiles" such as Hans Scharoun, and émigrés such as Ludwig Hilberseimer. A large proportion of the texts make reference to Northern Europe.[46] Fred Forbat contributes an article on urban planning laws in Sweden – an issue that aroused great interest among many architects who regretted the "missed opportunities" of the fainthearted land policy during reconstruction.[47] Hubert Hoffmann is among the most prolific contributors to the volume. Hoffmann had worked for Forbat in the late 1920s. In the 1940s he worked with Göderitz and Rainer on the *Gegliederte und aufgelockerte Stadt*. He was involved in the conception of the exhibition Die Stadt von Morgen and he designed, together with Wassili Luckhardt, a four-story apartment complex for the Interbau. Hoffmann contributes an essay on town planning in England, the Nordic countries, France, etc., which discusses *Vällingby, Guldheden, Gustavsberg, Gröndal, Tapiola, Rosta, and Friluftstaden.*[48] More interesting, however, is his essay entitled *Die Idee der Stadtplanung* (The Idea of City Planning).[49] This is an appeal for planning with references to the Athens Charter and the Interbau "theses of the city of tomorrow." Here, Hoffmann demands, in view of the "recognition of the limits of freedom," that a system be developed that "inhibits individual freedom as little as possible and fulfils [...] communal requirements." He claims that the "depression of the soul [...] in the mass-housing quarters of the city" forces us to recognize "the possibilities of positive psychological influence on people." Planning must provide "vessels" for an "amorphous" society, "within which and through which it can find a form again: the division into city units, areas, neighborhoods, and groups" similar to the "village community." Such "operations" have to be approached through "scientific and speculative, anticipatory and provisional action." For Hoffman, this can be seen in the Nordic countries. There, something that is "an essential prerequisite for planning: a community spirit" still exists, a "medieval shrewdness" which "can be observed

46 See Erich Kühn: "Städtebauliche Leitbilder," in: Vogler und Kühn: *Medizin und Städtebau*, vol. 2, pp. 563-574. On p. 567 it says that Denmark was "leading in the building trade." The settlements *Voldparken* in Husum, *Bredalsparken* in Hvidovre and *Fortunbyn* in Kongens Lyngby also appeared here.

47 Fred Forbat: "Städtebaugesetzgebung in Schweden," in: ibid., pp. 586-593.

48 Hubert Hoffmann: "Realisierungen der 'Neuen Stadt,'" in: ibid., pp. 620-640.

49 Hubert Hoffmann: "Die Idee der Stadtplanung," in: ibid., pp. 214-246. Incidentally, this text is filled with little jibes at what Hoffman considered Reichow's formalist organicism.

particularly in Scandinavia" and which makes possible the "active planning policies" in the North.[50]

Hoffmann's considerations stem from – to quote Zygmunt Baumann's definition of the modus operandi of social engineers – a gardener's habitus: the gardener sees his task in perfecting nature.[51] Hoffmann's anticipation of the future is expressed in a vocabulary that blends social order and biology. "Life is not hostile towards planning," says Hoffmann:

> You cannot compare life in society to a jungle where one plant takes away the light from the other. Our civilized environment rather seems to be similar to a garden, a plantation where a large part of the living conditions is dependent on artificial institutions. Just as the vine likes to climb up the pole that one lovingly offers it.[52]

Again, Hoffmann praises the open approach to planning that can be observed in England, Finland, and Sweden. But this time he also comments on the "abuse" of planning during the Nazi era: "Not only the bad, but first and foremost good instincts were lured and enlisted with psychological and scientific subtlety which then were used for criminal goals and materialistic ends."[53]

To sum up: all our texts develop a biological and/or sociological perspective on mankind as a basis of their planning, and they discover examples for this kind of planning in Northern Europe. Be it land policy or neighborhood unit, be it the ideal of the community or the aesthetics of the moderate Modernity: in the North, goals seemed to have been achieved that architects and urban planners had been striving for even before 1945. As experts, they considered the North to be the proof of the practicability of their intentions. Scandinavian moderation was regarded as result of planning which had organized society harmoniously.

50 Ibid., pp. 214f., p. 219, 221-224, 217, 225.

51 On this interpretation, see also Niels Gutschow: *Ordnungswahn. Architekten planen im "eingedeutschten Osten" 1939-1945*, Basel: Birkhäuser, 2001, p. 14.

52 Hoffmann: "Idee der Stadtplanung," p. 238.

53 Ibid., p. 239, 241.

The reference to the North can neither be reduced to the transfer of legal, administrative or technical knowledge, nor to an aesthetic and political "Westernization" or "liberalization."[54] Instead, it stemmed from a transnational Ordnungsdenken that was compatible with quite heterogeneous esthetical and political conventions of its time. It is not surprising that some theoreticians considered it an ethnic streak: Rudolf Hillebrecht said in the 1980s on the *Gegliederte und aufgelockerte Stadt* that it consisted of "basically Anglo-Saxon-Scandinavian ideas."[55] Hans Scharoun distinguished – again in *Medizin und Städtebau* – between a Germanic "culture" with its need for community building and a Roman "civilizing" way of thinking. Scharoun propagated building in correspondence to the "organic principle," a harmonious "social [...] principle of order" fundamentally tied to the "Nordic man."[56]

About the author

David Kuchenbuch is research associate on the project "Ordnungsdenken und *social engineering* als Reaktion auf die Moderne. Nordwesteuropa, 1920er bis 1950er Jahre" at the University of Oldenburg; he is preparing a dissertation entitled "Die Ordnung des Wohnraums. Ordnungsdenken und social engineering in Architektur und Stadtplanung, Deutschland und Schweden 1920er bis 1960er Jahre," and was involved in the interdisciplinary research network "Kulturelle Differenzierungen von Gesundheit und Krankheit in Wohlfahrtsstaaten" (in association with the Department for Northern European Studies at the Humboldt University Berlin, the Institute for Future Studies, Stockholm, and Örebro University).

54 See Anselm Doering-Manteuffel: "Westernisierung. Politisch-ideeller und kultureller Wandel in der Bundesrepublik bis zum Ende der 60er Jahre," in: Axel Schildt et al. (eds.): *Dynamische Zeiten. Die 60er Jahre in den beiden deutschen Staaten,* Hamburg: Christians, 2000, pp. 311-341; Ulrich Herbert: "Liberalisierung als Lernprozeß. Die Bundesrepublik in der deutschen Geschichte – eine Skizze," in: Ulrich Herbert (ed.): *Wandlungsprozesse in Westdeutschland. Belastung – Integration – Liberalisierung 1945-1980,* Göttingen: Wallstein, 2002, pp. 7-49.

55 "Ich kann mich nicht herausdenken aus dem Vorgang der Geschichte, in den ich eingebunden bin. Erinnerungen an den Wiederaufbau in der Bundesrepublik: Hintergründe, Leitbilder, Planungen. Max Guther, Rudolf Hillebrecht, Heinz Schmeissner, Walther Schmidt im Gespräch mit Werner Durth," in: *Stadtbauwelt,* no. 72, 1981, pp. 346-380, p. 377.

56 Hans Scharoun: "Ordnungsprinzipien und Begriffe, welche zu einer Stadtstruktur zu führen vermögen," in: Vogler and Kühn: *Medizin und Städtebau,* vol. 2, pp. 165-171, p. 166, 168.

THE NORDIC WAY TO MODERNITY

THE POLITICAL HISTORY OF THE NORDIC MODEL

Bernd Henningsen

[1]*A "Nordic Model"?*

Until well into the nineteenth century, the democratic model of politics in the Nordic countries developed along similar lines to other Western countries. Adopting Jewish, ancient/classic, and Christian ideas on the proper organization of social life, the political regimes were cautiously liberalized and democratized in the nineteenth century. In the process, the legal bases of the Middle Ages represented an important storehouse of tradition, which was furthermore called upon: no one may be imprisoned without judgment; the law is the basis of politics as formulated in the law of Jutland and the handbindings, both of which limited arbitrary rule by the monarchs. Interestingly, absolutism in Denmark and Scandinavia developed somewhat differently to the continent insofar as they had a specific term for the sovereignty of the divinely-ordained king: *Enevælde,* essentially meaning "sole rule"; an association with "despotism" is neither admissible, nor does it reflect political reality. The maltreatment of persons in the early modern age was not unknown in this society, but it took on a very different form south of the Eider river.

The absolutist regimes then collapsed in the early nineteenth century in Sweden (1809) and Norway (1814), Denmark granted itself a liberal-democratic constitution in 1849 – the most liberal and democratic of the time – parliamentarianism was introduced in Norway in 1884 and in Denmark in 1901, and with the independence of Norway in 1905, Finland in 1917, and Iceland in 1918, the present-day states were formed. At the end of the First World War, the party systems, parliamentarianism, the right to vote, and also the nationalization movements had in the North also already developed into the forms we know today.

As indicated, this pattern follows the temporal and factual events of European political history fairly exactly. However, the notion of a *special* form of democracy, of a Nordic political "model," which differs from others and yielded a unique, more humane form of society took root, not least in the Scandinavian countries themselves. The idea of a *distinct* democratic tradition, which allegedly contrasts with political

1 The following provides a condensed version of what I have written elsewhere in more detail about Denmark, see Bernd Henningsen: *Dänemark,* München: Beck, 2009 [series *Die Deutschen und ihre Nachbarn,* ed. by Helmut Schmidt and Richard von Weizsäcker].

reality in the South, is particularly cultivated by EU skeptics and opponents in the North. Society and politics are seen as egalitarian in orientation, more democratic, more peaceful. This self-assessment is not new but runs through political and intellectual history. In joining this European Community, women would forfeit their social rights and achievements, the welfare state would be cut back, national sovereignty would have to make way for outside influences controlled by capital, and so on.[2]

For this reason, it is also worth investigating the question of what the model diagnosis is based on, whether there are recognizable special qualities in Nordic politics that argue for the accuracy of the model label. Is speaking of a "special Nordic way," more harmonious and humane, justified? In the following, I will particularly turn my attention to the case of Denmark, which in a paradigmatic way also covers both the other Scandinavian countries – whereby it should be born in mind that in times of the welfare state and under social democratic dominance, Sweden considered itself the moral political conscience of the world, or was otherwise described as such in the discourse of identity.

The outstanding peculiarity of the Nordic countries in modern history is their unblemished political continuity. Although the Scandinavian countries also experienced the political and above all economic and social upheavals of the modern age, these took a far more moderate form here: the history of European revolutions was carried out elsewhere. In their characteristic features, the political regimes have not changed since the beginning of the twentieth century.

The history of Scandinavian mass emigration to America in the nineteenth century, the disappearance of entire social strata from society in only a couple of decades around the turn of the twentieth century – for example the *husmænd* in Denmark and Norway or the *torpare* in Sweden – and the economic shifts in the course of industrialization are, in themselves, huge intrusions into the respective histories, but

2 On the analysis of this self-image, see Carsten Schymik: *Europäische Anti-Föderalisten – Volksbewegungen gegen die Europäische Union in Skandinavien,* Leipzig/ Berlin: Edition Kirchhof and Franke, 2006; Uffe Østergaard: *Europa. Identitet og identitetspolitik,* Copenhagen: Rosinante, 2000 and 2002. On the early appeal to 'democratic' traditions, see Ingvar Andersson: "Äldre demokratisk tradition i Norden och dess fortsatta utforming i Sverige," in: Hal Koch and Alf Ross (eds.): *Nordisk Demokrati,* Kopenhagen: Westermann, 1948, pp. 5-39; see also Klaus von Beyme: *Die parlamentarischen Regierungssysteme in Europa,* München: Piper, 1973, pp. 29-34.

compared to other countries, their dimensions are rather marginal: industrialization in England claimed far more victims, political modernization in France reached far deeper. If the process of industrialization alone is compared, it is noticeable that, with its lack of raw materials, the Danish industrial landscape appears almost aseptic: no coal, no ore – no fumes, no dirt, the sun was and remains always visible.[3]

Ideological Immunity

The unbroken development of this northern European history is only explicable in an overall European context. Insofar as the Scandinavian societies particularly distinguish themselves from the other European societies by the fact that no ideological mass movements have arisen in the last 200 years, we are here dealing with a kind of ideological immunity:[4] while both left-wing and right-wing political movements developed into mass phenomena in almost all European countries from the end of the nineteenth century, Nordic lands were hardly infected by these ideologies at all. Although communist and fascist parties did exist there, they never managed more than the most marginal election results. Even at the zenith of Hitler's abuse of power, National Socialism remained a peripheral phenomenon; and in Finland, where in Scandinavian context the highest figures were reached, the popularity of the Communist Party after the Second World War never sufficed for more than a fifth of votes.

What is special about the Nordic democracies is not just that the political and cultural elites were unanimous in their rejection of ideological movements, but that this aversion is also reflected in the voting behavior of the people. This view can be adopted with qualifications: there were and are, of course, political utopias in the idea flows of the Nordic societies which feed off European messianic and Gnostic thought. However, a positive insistence on individualism, evolutionism, and empiricism was and remains predominant. In the political programs of the major parties or

3 On the history of industrialization in Norway, see Edvard Bull: *Sozialgeschichte der norwegischen Demokratie,* Stuttgart: Klett, 1969.

4 On Scandinavian immunity to ideologies, see Bernd Henningsen: *Die Politik des Einzelnen: Studien zur Genese der skandinavischen Ziviltheologie,* Göttingen: Vandenhoeck und Ruprecht, 1977.

in everyday political activity, the boundary of romantic eschatological thought has not been crossed (the late 1960s also mark a boundary line for the Nordic countries). Even those parties categorized as "radical" tend to emphasize "reformation" over "revolution"; from Holberg via Grundtvig to the social democratic welfare politicians of the postwar period in Norway, Sweden, and Denmark, the principle of a "focus on the people" was applied. It was not only the Anglo-Saxon countries that were spared the process of systematic rigorous thought derived from "reality" that lead the Italian, Spanish, German, even the Polish and other Eastern European nations to a history of fissures, but also the Nordic lands.

Politically, socially, and culturally, the Nordic countries present a region of extraordinary homogeneity, both in historical perspective and from the European viewpoint; only in most recent times with immigration from the south of Europe, the Middle and Far East, and not least from Africa, has this changed, although historical homogeneity is a fundamental underlying tenet of Nordic societies:

- Except for Finland, the Nordic countries are part of *one* language family, the North Germanic; it is *possible* to communicate with one another, semicommunication is in principle possible.
- With regard to ethnicity, there is barely a European region of comparable expanse which is so ethnically uniform. If the Germans in South Jutland, the Sami in Norway, Sweden, and Finland, the Swedes in Finland, and the Finns in Sweden are disregarded, there are, at least in historical perspective, no ethnic variants of significance in Northern Europe. Indeed, the fact that ethnic minorities existed at all only occurred to the general public in the 1970s, at a time of increased migration – to that extent, ethnic homogeneity has become a "qualified truth."
- An essential reinforcement of this linguistic and ethnic homogeneity is religious homogeneity. Relatively late, and relatively liberal converts to Christianity, the switchover from Catholicism to Protestantism in the sixteenth century was absolute – a "revolution from above" in the classical sense. A Counter-Reformation barely took place, so that a generous 90 percent of the population could be assumed to be of the Lutheran faith. Here too, "mass immigration"

since the 1970s created changes. However, Protestantism remains one of the most important pillars of the Nordic democracies.

This list of areas of homogeneity in the Nordic countries acquires a distinct political dimension if an attempt is made to compare them with other countries: a "minorities debate" did not have to take place – a "Sudeten German" problem could not arise; a language dispute, with the exception of Norway, was absent – a "Belgian" schism did not have to happen; the religious struggle was omitted – Northern Europe was not subject to an "Irish" problem. These political, social, and cultural homogeneities in the region and the respective countries thus contributed quite considerably to the stability and continuity of the Northern European countries.

The diagnosis of societal, political, and cultural homogeneity must naturally be relativized, as considerable heterogeneities lie concealed in the intranational and international common ground. These are typically not noticed by non-Scandinavians; for them, these differences and rivalries are hidden behind the obvious unity in political and societal reality which can be demonstrated with reference to a range of parameters. For me, the internal Scandinavian culture of humor is always a gauge of the rivalries, heterogeneities, and diverse national environments central to the development of specific ideas of Nordic democracy that stem from a remarkable process, in European context, of *nation building*. Even if the European parallels and congruencies are striking, the process still takes a different course here. The development of nationalism in

Europe and the nation building process are inextricably linked with national unity movements – in Germany, for example, initially in the Napoleonic Wars of Liberation, then the Paulskirche Movement of 1848, and the Bismarckian foundation of the German Reich in 1871. Pan-Germanism led to the "Lesser German Solution" with the creation of a unified German economic area, an independent flag, a German capital, and army, ultimately a fleet – within a relatively federalistic overall regime. At the same time, there was an analogous process in Italy, at the end of which, in 1864, a united Italy stood with Florence as its transient capital.

The conditions for these national building processes were also present in Scandinavia. A powerful, strongly appealing, initially cultural and then political movement of Scandinavianism arose in the second and third decades of the nineteenth century, but then, with the Danish national catastrophe, led to the stabilization of three nations, of which one – disregarding the case of Finland, which developed somewhat differently – first appears as an independent power on the international stage in 1905: Norway. Scandinavianism did not end with the creation of a unified Scandinavian national state within a geographically defined area with Stockholm (or Copenhagen) as capital, a swedenized Scandinavian national language, a uniform army and a unified overall flag, but in particularism as we know it today. The nineteenth century experienced Scandinavianism not as a unity movement but as the swedenization of Sweden, the denmarkization of Denmark, the norwegianization of Norway, the finlandization of Finland. If Scandinavianism had led to a success comparable to Germany or Italy, Europeans would have been proved right in their present-day homogeneity view of the North – which had, however, already existed in the nineteenth century. History, as we know, took a different course.

On the one hand, the national self-assertion of the Nordic (partial) nations took place against the backdrop of the homogeneity outlined above, on the other, it made an emphasis on the respective political and cultural differences necessary, which in turn were reinforced by precisely this emphasis and its consolidation in cultural memory. The missed opportunity for cohesion in the nineteenth century – which was in fact based on historical experience and centuries-old dreams – became a self-fulfilling prophecy.

Homogeneity and Continuity

Discussion of ruptures in political history is very important, because a considerable portion of the essential traits of Nordic democracies can be explained by political, historical, and institutional continuity – and vice versa: the continuity of institutions and the regime fundamentally explains political and national identity, the concordance of citizens with their government. To be added to this political continuity is the continuity in the nations' flow of ideas. When the modern nation states crystallized at the end of the eighteenth century and the beginning of the nineteenth century, they did so on the bases of their respective histories, their respective literatures and mythologies. The discovery of the *self* thus resulted in large part from the discovery of the *other*. For Denmark, the antagonistic others were the Swedes. With the ending of the eighteenth century, but especially in the twentieth century, the Germans assumed this role. The tiresome certainty that we are different to our neighbors may not be new but has become highly politicized since the Romantic age, as since then, we have been "better" than the *others*.

Continuity in political history is preceded by the continuity of the intellectual *construction* of continuity: before we can say what we are and will be, we must know what we were. For this reason, the idealists and romantics after the French Revolution were in search of the political roots, national literature, mythology, and roots of their own languages. From this historical, previously unordered material, they invented a continuity which stretches from the past, via the present, to the future. This is the basis of national identity: a cultural construction from a range of materials that are *explained* as essential at the respective current point in time.[5]

This construction of continuity works if the plausibility of the construction makes sense to the individual, if the materials are original and indigenous, if – and this defines the interaction between continuity and construction – they can be seamlessly integrated within the current experience of citizens. This was the case in the Nordic countries, as also in France and England: Nordic mythology and literature was original, as were the languages; above all, however, history was the treasure chest for the national construction of identity. This precisely describes Ernest Renan's definition of the nation at the end of the nineteenth century: a referendum on belonging that takes place every day.[6] Because the citizen identifies with society's image of itself, he thus identifies himself with his nation and is less likely to resort to surrogate identities, ideologies.

5 For more on the following, see Bernd Henningsen: "Johann Gottfried Herder und der Norden. Elemente eines Konstruktionsprozesses," in: Petra Huse and Ingmar Dette (eds.): *Abenteuer des Geistes – Dimensionen des Politischen. Festschrift für Walter Rothholz*, Baden-Baden: Nomos, 2008, pp. 85-101.

6 Ernest Renan: "Was ist eine Nation?" [Rede, 1882], in: *Was ist eine Nation? und andere politische Schriften*, ed. by Walter Euchner and Silvio Lanaro, Wien/ Bozen: Folio, 1995, pp. 41-58, p. 57.

Essential to the characterization of the politico-cultural environment is a social and cultural phenomenon, which, emanating from Denmark, must rank as typical of the Nordic countries and has had a sustainable impact: the popular movements since the end of the eighteenth century. They first developed as religious revivalist movements – with the Methodist John Wesley (1703-91) as the English example here – and accumulated in Scandinavia from the mid-nineteenth century: these movements need not be recounted to a Nordic audience, but are less known in the South. The fact that the revivalist, abstinence, workers', women's, anti-nuclear, and of course the adult education movements are counted as "popular movements" may be somewhat alien to, say, a German audience; here, they are considered as something exotic in social and political life.[7] They form an integral constituent of social and political life, a special hallmark of the democratization process since the nineteenth century, which still characterizes democracy today. They arose as a mass mobilization in the evolutionary process of modern democracies; through them, peasants and other lower classes learned to articulate themselves, to discuss, to handle contradictions, indeed in large part they first learned to read and write from them. They formed an attempt to reduce the educational gap between citizen and peasant, between city and country.[8]

The religious revivalist movements were followed by others. Nikolai Frederik Severin Grundtvig's adult education movement is one of the most enduring.[9] Two experiences fundamentally prompted Grundtvig's education concept: on the one hand, his
bad experiences with what he termed black pedagogy – the cultivation of grammar schools that imparted theoretical knowledge and in his opinion fostered no practical abilities for life – on the other, the experience that, at the beginning of the democratic age in which he lived and worked, the education gap between peasants or those who lived in the country and city-dwellers or citizens could only be made up for by special pedagogical institutions for precisely these social classes. Christen Kold (1816-70)

7 I offer a brief discussion of the Swedish case in: Bernd Henningsen: *Der Wohlfahrtsstaat Schweden*, Baden-Baden: Nomos, 1986, pp. 235ff.

8 See Henningsen: *Die Politik des Einzelnen*, pp. 33-39.

9 On the following see ibid., pp. 160-175.

borrowed the idea and founded the first so-called folk high school, *(folkehøjskole)*, in the South Jutland German-Danish border area during the conflict of national groups from 1848 on, which would soon be followed by further such institutions.

In the truest sense of the word, the adult students here learned *weltanschauung:* reading, writing, sums, singing, and praying. Later, the folk high schools also assumed the economic education of the peasants and influenced the education concepts and strategies of the cooperative movement. However, it was far more important that the common man in these institutions, as in all popular movements, learned to use the word, to discuss, and tolerate argument and criticism. The point of departure for the Danish notion of democracy, as formulated after several decades of positive experience in the twentieth century by theologian Ejler Løgstrup (1905-81) can be found here: democracy is a respectable way to be of a different opinion.

One can justifiably say that Grundtvig's adult education movement brought education that could be put to good use to the broad masses. Up to today, the movement and activists are characterized by their cultivation and use of the free word. Coined by him, the concept of the "living word" is used in Grundtvigian everyday life: at events, people really *speak,* rather than *read.*

The fact that the popular movements in the nineteenth century became the schools of democracy should also be placed in the context of the fact that the Nordic countries are world leaders in literacy: in no other world region was the degree of literacy in the population so high as here; nowhere else was this level attained as in the north of

Europe. The latest results thus also stem from a long and deeply rooted educational tradition: in the UN Human Development Index, which compares 179 countries with regard to such things as life expectancy and level of education in addition to GDP, Iceland and Norway rank as first and second, Sweden as seventh, Denmark as thirteenth, while Germany follows in only twenty-third place.[10]

10 United Nations Development Programme, Human Development Reports, http://hdr.undp.org/en/statistics/ [available 2.01.2009]

Folkelighed

In this context, Grundtvig's most central concept must be addressed, namely that of the *folkelighed*[11] – a word that defies translation, alone as a result of the misguided translations in times when racial purity had gained currency, and because all terms that reference the "people" are contaminated in German on account of this political past: *völkisch, Volkstümlichkeit, Volkstum, Volkheit,* etc. What Grundtvig meant is the experience of community and both political and social responsibility based on history, literature, but also the existence of the individual. It seems to me that the most suitable transcription may take its leave from Abraham Lincoln: "*of* the people, *by* the people, *for* the people."

With Grundtvig's *folkelighed,* Danish political identity is clearly isolated. Up to the present day, it is one of the central themes in Danish political debate. The folkelighed concerns everything "Danish": the myths, the history, the language, the common experience of the nation, the norms and values of this society. Grundtvig's thought may be inconceivable without its antagonism to its German – and Roman! – pendant and has hardly been sufficiently described, but at the same time its dependence on German philosophy is always deducible: Herder, Schelling, Schiller, Fichte must be mentioned here. He was familiar with Schleiermacher, Kant, Lessing, Hegel, Strauß, and it is always romanticism that remains his reference point. The historian, translator, and above all poet, Grundtvig drew lifelong strength from the harmonizing, optimistic worldview of the romantics. As a thinker, he never fathomed the romantic-speculative striving for unity but rather insisted on the contrast of dualities: truth and untruth, light and dark, life and death. He despised Italian-Roman culture, "May God liberate us from Rome," he proclaimed; by contrast, he saw promise in Ancient Greek and Nordic thought.

Grundtvig, the popular theologian, liberal politician, and parliamentarian, was a member of the Assembly of 1848/49 that gave rise to the basic law and a democratic constitution for Denmark. With his adult education movement, which was initially established in contrast to German incarnations in the mid-nineteenth century in

11 On the following, see Henningsen: *Die Politik des Einzelnen,* pp. 161ff.

South Jutland and would become an important vehicle for the democratization and parliamentarization of the country, anti-German sentiment also became an established factor of Danish political identity. Grundtvig's political vision of German arrogance was instrumentalized in the second half of the century, more than ever in the course of war in 1864, and ultimately became a fixed component of Danish civil theology in the twentieth century. Who knows whether the Danish image of Germany would have been different if the Germans had behaved better towards Denmark?

However, Grundtvig's significance for Denmark stretches far beyond this aspect; the name Grundtvig is associated with the central concepts of his theological and pedagogic thought: "joyful Christianity," "pioneers of freedom," "a school for life," "the living word." His three sojourns in England (1829-31) and his encounter with liberal English thought inspired his political, and not least his ecclesiopolitical, actions: "Initially with regard to freedom, as for everything human, I first learned in England to attach all importance to reality, with deep disdain for empty being and for ingratiation and bookworm existence in all its forms."[12] Grundtvig's liberalism was not individualistic, derived from the French tradition, rather he also incorporated a social, a societal component: state power should supply the frame within which the individual might freely develop.

While dominant liberalism demanded the dissolution of enduring absolutism and wanted to pass over to rigid majority rule, Grundtvig appealed for restrictions on all rule. This may at times read highly conservatively, even anti-democratically, but it has its corrective in the deep conviction of the status equality of individuals, who in competition with one another are in a position to discover general prosperity. "Freedom to make use of his gift without interfering in the absolute rights of others, freedom to do what does not dispute the laws of morals or of civil reason – is desirable."[13] Not just "freedom of conscience, but above all freedom of competition" was his objective. According to his principles, the "best of all" has its origins in helping oneself.

12 Nikolai Frederik Severin Grundtvig: *Udvalgte Skrifter*, ed. by Holger Begtrup, 10 vols., Copenhagen: Gyldendalske Boghandel, 1904-09, vol. 10, 1909, p. 356.

13 Grundtvig: *Udvalgte Skrifter*, vol. 1, 1904, pp. 52f.

What is Democracy?

Hal Koch (1904-63), from 1937 Professor of Ecclesiastical History at Copenhagen University and a central figure in the Danish cultural canon[14] – the reason for a brief explanation of his "Danish" concept of democracy at this juncture – calls the folk high schools "practical schools of democracy."

> Here, "people learned what it means [...] to negotiate; they learned to understand other viewpoints and come to terms with them, above all they learned the art of cooperation, they learned, to a certain degree, to see the interests of the whole."[15]

The "living word" can also be detected in Koch's most well-known publication, the slender volume edited in 1945 entitled, *What is Democracy?* Socrates, Plato, and Grundtvig are its most often quoted authorities. Koch presents democracy as a way of life, an attitude, not safeguarded by institutional or legal guidelines but by enlightenment and education. After the end of German occupation, Koch opposed the legal assessment of the dictatorship and the sentencing of tacit supporters. Armed with classical philosophy and Grundtvig, he took an opposing stance to his legal colleague Alf Ross (1899-1979), who represented the contradictory view (Ross was a prominent representative of "Scandinavian legal positivism" and the Danish representative at the European Court of Human Rights from 1959 to 1972). Enlightenment and educational work in the spirit of Grundtvig was, for Koch, the only truly effective tool to counter Nazification of the population. Democracy means dialog – Socratic dialog –, communication, mutual respect, and understanding. If it requires a vote, the democratic principle has already lost. In fact, it is probably one of the characteristics of the Danish notion of democracy that voting is avoided, that consensus arises through dialog. This does not rule out the possibility that this consensus is sometimes also truly democratic.

14 Kulturministeriet (ed.): *Kulturkanon*, Copenhagen: Politikens Forlag, 2006. A new biography presents an account of Koch's life and work, as well as his political and cultural environment. See Jes Fabricius Møller: *Hal Koch en biografi*, Kopenhagen: Gads Forlag, 2009.

15 Hal Koch: *Hvad er demokrati?* Copenhagen: Gyldendal, 1960 [1945], p. 42.

With the development and formulation of the civil theological folkelighed, with its institutionalization in folk high schools, and the ever continuing debate around the folkelighed, Grundtvig has become an outstanding representative of the Danish understanding of politics. In the conscious recourse to the common Western tradition of political thought – Jewish-Mosaic, Ancient Greek, Christian-Protestant, and then also Nordic – he articulates a form of consciousness that could be characterized as Danish-Nordic and became the basis of a national identity. With this, the tradition I made reference to at the top of this brief overview would have come full circle, also expressing the remarkable aspects of Scandinavian political awareness.

With this interpretation, I have more or less observed official Grundtvig reception. Regardless of where one enters the discourse of authoritative interpretation of Danish identity, Grundtvig is always placed on the altar of civil theology as father of the nation. Grundtvig is mentioned in the Danish democratic canon – the ministerially approved basic law for Danish political and democratic understanding[16] – in just this harmonious context. However, like its neighbors, Denmark has experienced a number of identity crises in the last forty years. This began with the 1968 movement, continued with the political mobilization arising from the Europe debates from the 1970s; the sensed threat to the specifically "Danish" from modern immigration then further muddled societal self-understanding of the valid and traditional values of this society. To that extent, Grundtvig has certainly become a father figure for the younger generations, called on at best where many would most like to see fathers: in the museum.

About the author
Bernd Henningsen is professor of Scandinavian and cultural studies as well as culture and politics of Northern Europe and the Baltic Region at the Department for Northern European Studies at the Humboldt University Berlin; (founding) director of the Department for Northern European Studies; visiting and guest professor at the University of Minnesota in Minneapolis (USA), Zurich, Hamburg, Trier, Erlangen-Nürnberg, and the Free University Berlin; 2002-03 professor of political science, culture and politics in Northern Europe and the Baltic Sea Region at Ernst-Moritz-Arndt University; visiting professor at Södertörn University College (Stockholm), Örebro University, and the University of Copenhagen; relevant publications include *Die Politik des Einzelnen. Zur Genese der skandinavischen Ziviltheologie* (1977) and *Der Wohlfahrtsstaat Schweden* (1986).

16 Kulturministeriet: *Kulturkanon.*

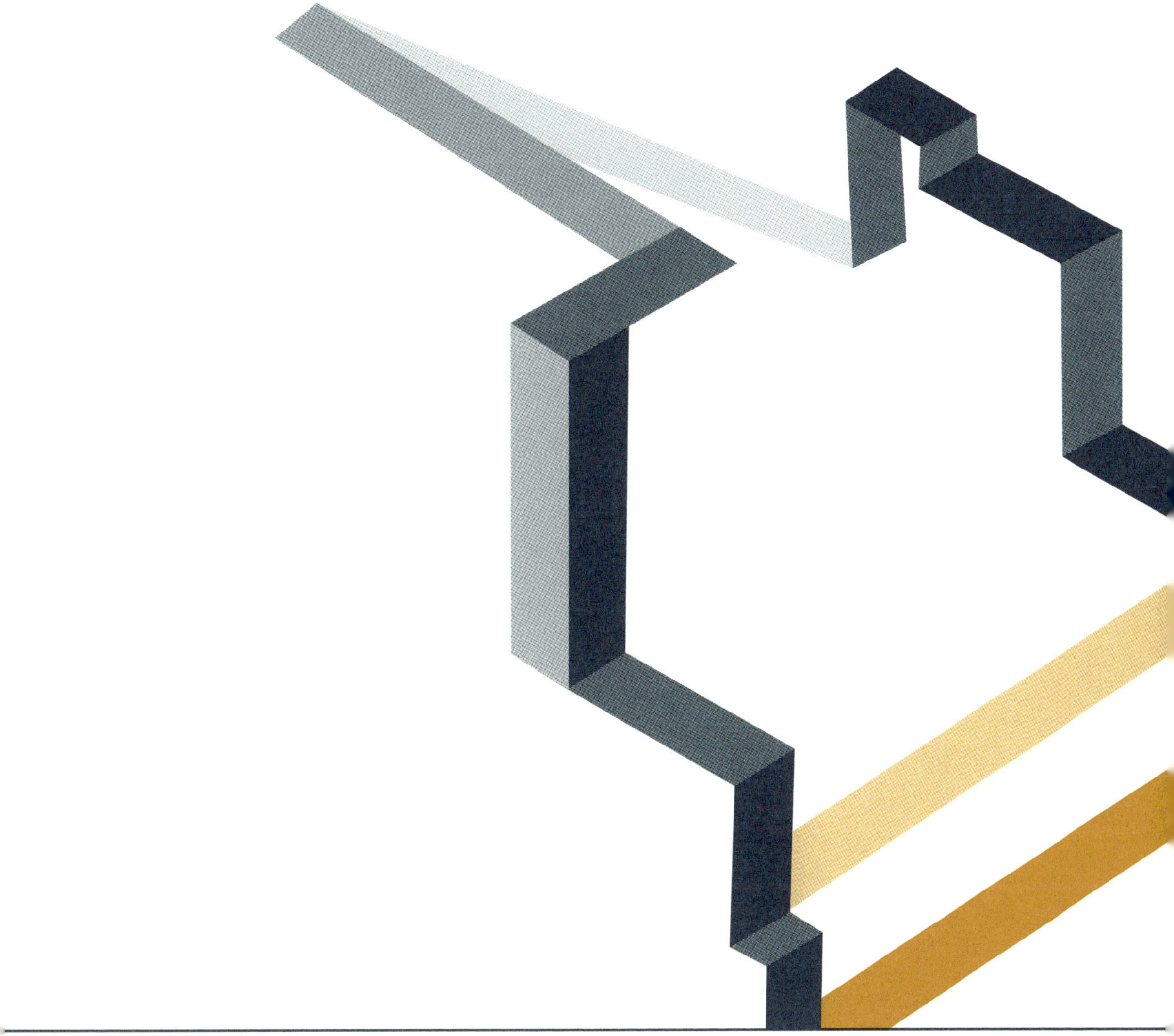

THE STRUCTURE OF DESIRE

THE IDEOLOGICAL MOTIVES OF SWEDISH MODERNISM AND THE ROAD TO THE "PEOPLE'S HOME"

Sven-Olov Wallenstein

The introduction of modernist architecture and design in Sweden was marked by two highly significant events, the 1930 Stockholm Exhibition and the publication in 1931 of the first manifesto, *Acceptera.* The use of the verb "accept," hovering somewhat indeterminately between an infinitive and an imperative form (although the latter takes precedence as the text unfolds), appears to indicate what is at stake: modernism and modernity must be accepted as an unavoidable historical force, and the role of subjective response can only be to acquiesce to the powers that be. This reading is, however, not entirely justified; in fact, a considerable amount of intellectual and rhetorical energy was spent on creating the possibility of identification, to forge a subjectivity that would not perceive the process of modernization as an external threat but rather as emanating both from within the subject itself and from a collective national history – both of which were to become characteristic features of the Swedish model and the emerging Social Democratic welfare state.

In this perspective, modernism must be seen as a process unfolding on the level of affects and desires, and it belongs to the dimension in which unconscious investments merge with social imperatives, and where a certain *jouissance* is produced in the intersection between individual and collective. Here, I would like to juxtapose the Swedish model with a similar way of negotiating desire and the collective: the visions of a reformed subjectivity in the Soviet avant-garde in the late 1920s, where the task was to make room for an erotic investment in things that would not solidify into fetishistic structures. Examining the subterranean links that unite these two positions (between which no direct influence, to my knowledge, can be discerned) might provide a different and more complex perspective on this historical phase, in which many of the parameters that would determine the course of modern architecture were defined.

I. Desire, Consumption, and Subjectivity in Swedish Modernism

Co-written by six of the most prestigious Swedish architects and intellectuals of the time – Gunnar Asplund, Wolter Gahn, Sven Markelius, Gregor Paulsson, Eskil Sundahl, and Uno Åhrén – the manifesto *Acceptera* was published at a time when the European avant-garde was entering into a state of crisis. In Manfredo Tafuri's influential diagnosis, utopian modernism had already entered its final stage around 1930, as can be seen in the conflicts around the Siemensstadt project in Berlin. This, Tafuri says, is the place where "one of the most serious ruptures within the 'modern movement' became evident,"[1] and where the compromise between those architects whose aim was to save the "aura" (Scharoun and Häring) and those who consequently adopted the assembly line as their model (Gropius and Bartning) become impossible to solve. The idea of the plan, which for a moment seemed like the instrument that would finally allow architecture to attain its true completion, eventually absorbed all illusions of autonomy within the global economic restructuring that occurred in the wake of the Wall Street crash, when Keynes's *General Theory of Employment, Interest and Money* (1936) displaced the avant-garde manifesto as a way to project and plan the future. In this way, architecture becomes a mediating – but, as such, merely temporary – link between utopian projection and political realism, and Tafuri can, without further ado, propose a reading of the various avant-garde visions of the 1920s as so many failed attempts to provide formal solutions to problems whose answers could not be found on the level of design. Architects themselves were both unable and unwilling to draw such conclusions, and instead they experimented with their own formal tools in order to tackle issues that essentially belonged on the level of social organization as a whole.

But instead of seeing this as an ending point of modern architecture, would it not be just as possible to look at the kind of historical compromise between labor and capital – which for Tafuri formed the impossible horizon for a project like Ernst May's "Das neue Frankfurt" and whose formal contradictions exploded in Siemensstadt – as that which could become a different source of energy, and allow architecture and urban planning to become privileged instruments for the formation of a new type of subjectivity? The case of Sweden seems to warrant precisely this conclusion, and especially so when seen at the level of formation of subjectivity, fantasy, and desire.

1 Manfredo Tafuri: *Architecture and Utopia,* Cambridge, Mass.: MIT Press, 1976, translated by Barbara Luigi la Penta [Manfredo Tafuri: *Progetto e utopia,* Bari: Laterza, 1973], pp. 116f. For a discussion of the relation between Tafuri's version of modernism and the particularities of the Swedish development, see Helena Mattsson and Sven-Olov Wallenstein: 1930/31: *Swedish Modernism at the Crossroads/ Der schwedische Modernismus am Scheideweg,* Stockholm: Axl Books, 2009.

In fact, the decisive rhetorical strategy put to use in *Acceptera* seems always and systematically to assume two contradictory standpoints, so that a bridge between past and present can be created instead of an opposition between the modern breakthrough and the persistence of tradition. It is no doubt less useful to see this as lingering conservatism, simple cowardice, or as a compromise doomed in advance, as Tafuri would have it: it is in fact part of an overarching political strategy that has become predominant in the whole of Swedish modernity. If there is an obvious stress on social utility, one should pay just as much attention to the considerable energy spent on making individuals identify with the project of modernization, and, in this sense, the "compromise" is only a tactical move within a larger strategy. The Swedish model is undoubtedly "softer" than the European avant-garde, with its more or less utopian visions – more pragmatic, perhaps – but also much more efficient in the way that it gently intervenes in everyday life and restructures social relations. If Tafuri's "concrete politicizing" of architecture was a short-lived experiment in Europe, in Sweden it became one of the ideological cornerstones for the further development, and spirit of "mutual agreement," between labor and capital that had reigned ever since the legendary agreement between employers and trade unions in 1938 in Saltsjöbaden (the origin of the famous "spirit of Saltsjöbaden") – an agreement to which official recourse has most often been made in the reproduction of Social Democratic hegemony.

Now, my entry into this complex of ideas will be through the idea of *consumption:* what it means to desire a commodity, and in what way does the acquisition of new

(and old) items produce an environment in which we feel at ease? In what way does a transformed notion of both subject and object come into play in this new assemblage that in my reading constitutes one of the essential features of the modernist architectural project in this stage, and will continue to do so in the postwar period, in a transformed and intensified form?

In the discussion of *hemtrevnad* (coziness) in chapter six of *Acceptera,* which constitutes a response to imagined objections against the preceding chapter and its discussions of the standardization of housing, the authors ask if we in fact will need to sacrifice intimacy, emotional depth, and affective ties to our things, and the answer is an emphatic No. The *true* meaning of coziness, they suggest, is that everything is in its proper place, and that all the things that surround us contribute to a state of psychological well-being; in this, functionality in fact proves to be a precondition for psychological identification, and not at all an obstacle. It is precisely this functionality that will allow us to furnish our homes with the things that we really need, starting from an analysis of the lives that we in fact lead, and, in this sense, *stylistic unity* need not be decisive at all. Old objects still retain their emotional value and their place in our environment; instead, what matters is that all new things we acquire should not simulate a tradition of which they are not a part, but must facilitate our relation to the present. The authors emphasize that beauty can never arise from *untruth*, just as little as coziness can be bought:

> "Beauty can be achieved in many ways. But the false and untrue rarely become beautiful – in the long run, even though it may please for the moment. Beauty is not tied to any formal schema. It depends on the way in which a thing is done."[2]

This *false* desire for a simulated history is in fact generated by the speculative force of a market logic that operates through a personalization of the commodity that is fundamentally untrue.

> "In spite of the assurances to the contrary from smart advertising, who would believe that he can, for instance, buy a personal car or a personal broadcloth [...] let us remember that we cannot give the new the affective or emotional value of the old by mimicking it."[3]

It is indeed essential to get rid of bad craftsmanship, so that sound and genuine taste, honesty, authenticity, etc., may prevail, but not to discard the old as such.

As we can see, the important issue is not to be modern or to construct one's environment in an esthetically rigorous way, but to configure everyday life so that it becomes true, and so that every object comes to express its authentic *historical location*. In this

2 Gunnar Asplund et al. (eds.): *Acceptera*, Stockholm: Tiden, 1931, p. 103.

3 Ibid., p. 104.

patchwork milieu, old and new alike have their place, and in fact, the relaxed and confident way in which the old exerts its function can be taken as the paradigm for the *true* new, unlike the *false* new, which will always be marked by a certain temporal insecurity: neither past nor present, it is incapable of assuming a correct and truthful stance.

The same conception underlies the argument in the following chapter, "Industry and Craft." Here, too, the authors want to get rid of a certain set of presuppositions that have turned into clichés and consequently block the current development. The enemy is the outdated legacy of Ruskin and Morris, which was once a sound reaction but today has lead to the portrayal of the industrial commodity as somehow degraded and untrue, and introduced a spiral of false imitations that lead us to believe that the modern commodity needs to be "masked" in order not to look cheap. In the present, the authors argue, these arguments lead us astray; they hinder sound development and enhance the artificial production, of, for instance, "fake antiques." These imitations of historical objects are in fact cheap, while they are supposed to give the illusion of being precious, and in the end they lead to feelings of *emptiness* and *disgust*, even a profound sense of *shame:* "All the pretentious and false commodities that we now cherish will sooner or later reveal their emptiness and produce a sense of disgust. We feel ashamed and are dissatisfied with our credulousness."[4]

This shame must be taken as the starting point for a different type of analysis of desire, and the motto that we should give people what they want leads in the wrong

direction. Instead, it must be understood as the decisive task of a new type of intellectual to rethink this idea – for, the authors state without further ado, it is only *a select few who in fact know what they want.* This new analysis is based on the need for an "objective knowledge of the commodity," although this knowledge is at present only held by a small group, "normally the buyers at the larger firms."[5] Only this analysis can provide the foundation for a *natural* design of the commodity, i.e., the form that the commodity would take if it could be rescued from the fetishist logic that constitutes it precisely as a commodity. The thing must be freed from the speculative logic of the

4 Ibid., p. 108.

5 Ibid.

commodity and all the false desires that it engenders, not however in order to become pure use-value, but so that it may function as the support of a desire that would be contemporary with itself, as it were.

Elin Wägner, one of the most influential political writers and intellectuals of the period, speaks of the revolution of modern times not as a political event but as a change in perspective, a new way of looking at things that will bring about the "transition from individualism to collectivism."[6] By redefining the relation between the personal and the standardized, the consumer item as a representation of social status was to be re-functionalized so that it would express the possibility of a classless society. The question for this new linkage of type and personality then becomes: how can one make people desire that which is standardized? The first response to this is: through education and schooling, and here we can see the outlines of a typical project of emancipation through discipline. However, the second answer, which is particular to *Acceptera*, is that we must also reconnect to the tradition, and here, the "objective knowledge of the commodity" can be reinterpreted as an extension of the traditional formation of types that was already at work in the past. Paradoxically, the type is not primarily a result of modern, rationalized forms of production, or an answer to the general needs of a subject attuned to such forms, and if on one level it is a conscious striving for "communal forms," it is at the same time, and just as fundamentally, an expression of variety and personality.

In fact, the type is that which lies at the foundation of that part of our personality which expresses the universal, as was claimed in 1929 by one of the authors of *Acceptera,* Uno Åhren.[7] Personality has two parts, he suggests, the universal and the individual, and the first represents the "classless" object (the commodity outside of the logic of fetishism), while the second represents the consumer item in its "fake" form. In other words, individual taste can, quite easily, be satisfied through standardization to the extent that the consumer develops the universal side of his personality, all of which will lead to the formation of a subjectivity rooted in the collective. This reduces

6 Elin Wägner: "Revolution," in: *Svenska Slöjdföreningens tidskrift,* 1929, pp. 155-158, p. 155.

7 Uno Åhrén: "Standardisering och personlighet," in: *Svenska Slöjdföreningens tidskrift,* 1929, pp. 44-50.

the desire for false commodities, i.e., that which belongs to our individuality, and instead it engenders a structure of fantasy that allows us to see our necessary connection to a collective life process. In this sense, the commodity can pave the way for the individual's entry into the collective of the future by separating true and sound variations (natural type formations) from pointless ones (the morphological fluctuations of individualistic consumer items), and it integrates the moment of functionality into a process whereby the subject itself comes into being in a new fashion.

The tricky question, then, obviously becomes which needs should be assumed to be basic. It is tempting to reconstruct this discussion in quasi-Lacanian terms: How can we find a balanced articulation between *need*, which is somehow natural and anthropological; *demand*, which is the expression of needs in a given context, always subject to deviation and falsification by all kinds of external pressure mechanisms, for instance the speculative market logic that leads us to believe that we need something that we do not; and *desire*, the *difference* between need and demand, that which by its very essence is infinite since it is a *lack* that constitutes the very being of the subject, at the same a "lack-in-being" and a "lack-to-be"? How can such desire be put to work so that it reinstalls a balance between need and demand, and performs its cathexes on things that are conducive to the integration of the subject into the new symbolic order?

Some of these needs seem inescapable, the authors say, but we also imagine ourselves as having many more and diversified needs. The increase in production and the emergence of new needs are interdependent, and with advertising, the risk of "overstimulation" arises, a situation where the needs themselves will wind up being produced, which means that the infinity of desire takes precedence over the actual usefulness of the object, which now becomes nothing but an effect of a difference in a system of objects.[8] In the postwar period, such "induced desires" formed the bedrock of the new theory of marketing. This is also the project in *Acceptera*, even

8 This type of analysis developed in the early work of Jean Baudrillard, from *Le système des objets* (1968) to *Pour une critique de l'économie politique du signe* (1972). In Baudrillard's analysis, early modernism, for him exemplified by the Bauhaus, was the decisive step into the logic of the political economy of the sign, where exchange value begins to free itself from use value, and then reconstructs the latter as a mirage or fantasy. In my perspective, early modernism identifies this emerging logic and attempts to *contain* it by various techniques, and the successes and failures of such techniques.

though here it is carried out through the commodity and not through marketing. Whereas American industrial design and everything that would follow in its wake could be understood as a challenge to modernist conceptions, the Swedish debate did not interpret the individualism of commercial culture as an opposition to modernism, but instead proposed the idea of a tradition and a vernacular culture that was itself the bearer of true individual expression. In this sense, modernism could be projected as a continuation or a variation of a Swedish proto-functionalist program, rather than a break away from it. If postwar theories could claim that it is advertising that produces a consumer, in Swedish functionalism it is the very consumption of the commodity that produces the new consumer. The true issue is here to steer what Åhren calls an individualistic desire, and in this perspective the authors of *Acceptera* constantly attempt to define a moral and psychological limit between true and false desires, the everyday item and the superfluous luxury object.

The essence of the everyday item, they claim, resides in its utility and unassuming quality. It is "calm" and becoming, and reduces eloquence to a simple, true language, one that *serves*. "We must also recognize that the better someone serves, the less noise he makes. The everyday item should be useful, unassuming, calm, and becoming."[9] At the same time, this unassuming calm is always threatened by the value of representation and rhetoric, by the sheer verbosity of the commodity, and the difference that desire is always capable of introducing. For us moderns, the authors claim, luxury must be a question of quality, not of pomp – we are no longer dealing with the old kind of "barbaric luxury"; in fact, even this type of wasteful expenditure must now be subjected to the functional imperative. It need not be underscored that this is not a description of a new reality, but an attempt to conjure it up, to project it as an image: the issue is to educate and mold a future consumer, a subject that should desire abundance, luxury, and excess, but as internal moments of the function. True luxury, true excess, is that which displays an excess of functionality, that which is truly useful.

This is why the authors of *Acceptera,* in all their fascination with technological development, still underline incessantly that "man's spiritual needs" must not be forgotten, that is, we must not forget the essentiality of the creation of a mediating

9 *Acceptera,* p. 121.

position between the antagonistic poles of Expressionism and *Neue Sachlichkeit* in the European avant-garde. If, in the name of Taylorism and the assembly line, we have to accept structures implied by a technologically advanced division of labor, then we must not forget that this can lead to a higher satisfaction in a type of work that goes beyond the old crafts, and is at the basis of a new collective understanding of work. Eventually, the authors predict, a new and "higher type of man"[10] may arise from this collective work. And, in a cunning twist of the argument, they propose that if mass production and standardization are ways to raise quality, and if "Swedes are a people who value work oriented toward quality," this means that everything that seems to threaten the national heritage from the outside is in fact the true understanding of Swedishness, and in this sense it can be safely assumed that "we are better equipped than many other nations to promote aspirations toward quality in production."[11]

A similar perspective organizes the following discussion in the chapter "Form," which poses the question of how we can overcome the traditional distinction between technology and art. Today we have entered a new world of forms, which is no longer the same as it was during the first brutal phases of industrialism, and this creates a new cultural condition that makes it necessary to get rid of the old aesthetic paradigms. Opposing the hierarchy of the fine and applied arts, *Acceptera* asserts that utilitarian art has a beauty of its own, an evident and transparent form, an "intuitive Gestaltung" of the form-function complex rather than a "machine romanticism."[12] The Germans, they say, talk of this in terms of *Gestaltung von Lebensvorgängen,* the "shaping of life processes," in order to withdraw from "aesthetic debates with their endless nonsensical talk"[13] – but, they add, there is just as much nonsensical talk with respect to the practical sphere. Opposing both of these nonsensical discourses, they propose that "art is order," meaning, "an object displaying a perfect order and an unbroken continuity between form and function."[14] In this idea of order and organization we may of course see the ideological operation par excellence: a naturalization that also involves the

10 Ibid., p. 128.

11 Ibid., p. 128f.

12 Ibid., p. 139.

13 Ibid., p. 140.

14 Ibid.

"process of life" in its integrity, and postulates a continuity among object, function, and user that does not allow for further questions because it is intuitive, evident, and transparent. But to this argument, which is a variation on many similar tropes in the European debate, they add a link to a specific Swedish tradition in order to overcome the rift in the tradition opened up by such a rigorously rational and technocratic "shaping of life processes." An image of the Ornäs house, a classically Swedish rural type, is accompanied by a rhetorical outcry: "A new 'functional' building? No, the Ornäs house. The difference is no bigger than this."[15] The most Swedish of everything – history in its truth – is already on its way toward functionalism, even though the lack of industrial technology impeded the "natural formation of types" that was always there from reaching all the way to our modern standardization. When we build the new, we can rest assured that we are continuing to build on the past, as well as on its true significance. What disappears are the particular solutions and the specific "looks" of the past, not its inner truth.

There is indeed an easiness and lightness in the good old style – "the old Swedish rural art of building was just as natural, honest, and primitive as the rural population itself."[16] On the other hand, the recent past – the most degraded category of them all, since it points to the temporal quality of the *recently outdated* that has haunted fashion ever since it was formulated by Baudelaire – signifies a split, a fracture that leads us to "tinker around with old architectural fragments,"[17] with things that have lost their organic connection to time and constitute the very essence of untruth. It should be noted that the concept of "fashion" is not at all rejected in the text: the force of fashion is supposed to free us from eternal models, and to press onward along with time itself. To move ahead is also to move backward to the true roots; to return to the authentic tradition is to move ahead. This is the operation that is the foundation for a certain Swedish modernity, whose "pragmatism" and eagerness to "compromise" should not be seen as a defensive retreat from the radical stance of the European avant-garde, but as a move that here, at a crossroads in 1930/31, came to define the basic features of Sweden in the making.

15 Ibid., p. 144.

16 Ibid., p. 150.

17 Ibid., p. 151.

II. Constructing Desire

If we now turn our attention to Russian Constructivism, the differences seem at first hand to prevail. In traditional readings, it has indeed often been perceived as a thorough-going and even violent attempt to eradicate individuality and to produce a "new man" whose desires and affects would be wholly attuned to a technological and collective society.[18] Although this in many respects is a well-founded interpretation, dissenting voices within the avant-garde should also be acknowledged, and even though they would soon be eradicated or consigned to the margins of history, they provide us with a more complex image of the process of modernization, whose differences and particularities could become the starting point for an assessment of a constitutive *multiplicity* of modernities.

The unilateral and negative image is often based on the ideas of a "scientific organization labor" that was put forth by many theorists, for instance poet Aleksei Gastev, who was one of the founders of NOT (Institute for the Scientific Organization of Work) and the author of an influential book, *How To Work* (*Kak nado rabotat',* 1922), where a cult of the machine in the form of the assembly line and a Taylorized structuring of space and time were fundamental features. Gastev's proposals explicitly situate themselves as heirs to a whole series of classical disciplinary functions (the army, the prison, the church, etc.) that in his perspective need to be resuscitated as conscious instruments for the shaping of the population, and in this he clearly illustrates the thesis of a unidirectional and repressive modernization.

18 See for instance Hubertus Gassner: "The Constructivists: Modernism on the Way to Modernization," in: Solomon R. Guggenheim Museum, State Tretiakov Gallery, State Russian Museum, Schirn Kunsthalle Frankfurt (eds.): *The Great Utopia: The Russian and Soviet Avant-Garde, 1915-1932,* New York: Guggenheim Foundation, 1992, pp. 298-319; Manfredo Tafuri: "U.S.S.R.–Berlin 1922: From Populism to 'Constructivism,'" in: Tafuri: *The Sphere and the Labyrinth: Avant-Gardes and Architecture from Piranesi to the 1970s* (trans. by Pellegrino d'Acierno and Robert Connolly), Cambridge, Mass.: MIT, 1990; Boris Groys: *Gesamtkunstwerk Stalin,* München: Hanser, 1983. On the idea of a "New Man" and its connections to the avant-garde conception of technology, cf. the massive documentation assembled by Boris Groys et al. (eds.): *Am Nullpunkt. Positionen der russischen Avantgarde,* Frankfurt am Main: Suhrkamp, 2005, and *Die neue Menschheit. Biopolitische Utopien in Russland zu Beginn des 20. Jahrhunderts,* Frankfurt am Main: Suhrkamp, 2005.

Different models were however proposed, also from within the circle of Productivist theorists, for instance by Boris Arvatov, for whom the notion of "everyday life" *(byt)* was the key concept.[19] This was still an idea of a technical organization, although one that would not emanate from a transcendent will to power, but rather follow the rhythms of the collective, and allow for a different appreciation of the things themselves in their materiality and presence. The issue for Arvatov was to forge the idea of a "socialist object," a thing that would be not only functional but also malleable and responsive, and transcend the imperative of technological efficiency without being opposed to it. "Connected like a co-worker with human practice,"[20] the thing, in what appears like a strategic inversion of Marx's diagnosis of commodity fetishism, attains an agency of its own and assumes a capacity to restructure human relations in a more rational and open-ended fashion that respects our freedom.

It is by *using* objects in a certain way, and allowing them to enter into the subjective life process, and not by *producing* them, that we will be transformed, and here Arvatov provides a new take on the Productivist credo: his vision is a socialist culture that would equal Western capitalist modernity and yet be capable of engendering a different set of interpersonal relations that must overcome the division between labor and consumption.[21] Even mundane objects, Arvatov suggests, radiate a particular way of life that must become the object of analysis: "The ability to pick up a cigarette-case, to smoke a cigarette, to put on an overcoat, to wear a cap, to open a door, all these 'trivialities' acquire their qualification, their not unimportant 'culture.'"[22] Like many of his peers in the Russian avant-garde, Arvatov was attracted to things and products

19 See Boris Arvatov: "Everday Life and the Culture of the Thing (Towards the Formulation of the Question)," translated by Christina Kiaer, *October*, vol. 81, Summer 1997, pp. 119-121. In the following cited in the text with pagination. For a lucid commentary, see Kiaer's accompanying essay, "Boris Arvatov's Socialist Objects," in: ibid., pp. 105-118. For a translation of Arvatov's more harsh Productivist writing, see Arvatov: *Kunst und Produktion*, München: Hanser, 1972. For a discussion of the idea of byt, see also Svetlana Boym: *Common Places: Mythologies of Everyday Life in Russia*, Cambridge: Harvard University Press, 1994.

20 *Acceptera*, p. 126.

21 As Christina Kiaer notes, Arvatov's conception of everyday life does not imply resistance to a technological colonization of the life world, as will most subsequent analyses (Henri Lefebvre, Michel de Certeau), but the synthesis of these two levels ("Boris Arvatov's Socialist Objects," p. 114).

22 *Acceptera*, p. 126.

that radiate a technological modernity, but in pointing to the more subdued and low-key artifacts of everyday material culture, he underlined the importance of integrating a dimension of intimacy and affectivity, in order to overcome the divide between production and consumption within a "monism of Things."[23]

This new use and experience of things above all relates to their status as commodities. Unlike the bourgeois system, which isolates production from private and passive consumption and makes the thing into a "dead" entity, socialist everyday life should make the thing active, into a "co-worker."[24] In Arvatov's view, commodity fetishism does not so much render the object *pseudo-active* (as a displacement and concealment of true social relations, as Marx would say) as it makes it *passive,* and locates it "outside its creative genesis."[25] To rethink the thing is the task of a new "technical intelligentsia," which Arvatov sees emerging above all in the US, and whose experience of its own material culture is of a different kind (although the class origins of this emerging group sets limits to their self-understanding): they already understand the outlines of the collective nature of production, and have allowed this to enter into their own psychological set-up; they do not own the things they work upon, but organize them in their flows and movement. This is why they demand an active and flexible object, ready to be re-configured in the "montage" of new social practice, and discard the static and representational things of an earlier bourgeois culture.

The new "psycho-physiological individual" that is born out of such a new organizational logic should not be seen as the result of a mere process of discipline and coercion, but as the outcome of a much more complex process of "subjectivation" (to use Foucault's term) which integrates moments of response, agency, and freedom as inner moments in the production of a new type of subject.[26] In this way it would be far too simplistic to see this process *simply* in terms of a repression of desire, although there indeed is a certain repression at work; perhaps it would be more correct to speak

23 Ibid., p. 127.

24 Ibid., p. 124.

25 Ibid., p. 122.

26 For a discussion of Foucault's model in relation to the development of modern architectural theory, see my *Biopolitics and the Emergence of Modern Architecture,* New York: Princeton Architectural Press, 2009.

of a *conscious and controlled repression of repression,* or a fantasy of being able to contain the subject by *designing* a space of freedom and subjective latitude, which is what gives Constructivism its peculiar, at once sober and fantasmatic relation to technology.

This comes across in one of most publicized of the Constructivist projects, the Workers' Club that Rodchenko designed for the Russian Pavilion at the Exposition Internationale des Arts Décoratifs et Industriels in Paris 1925.[27] In its ascetic purity, Rodchenko's design may appear as little more than a low-tech Soviet version of a functionalist modernism, but as Christina Kiaer argues, the motivating force underlying this work is in fact much more complex and perhaps not even transparent to the artist himself. The shocking encounter with a fully developed Parisian modernity and its commodity fetishism (reflected in Rodchenko's letters to his family, which oscillate between disgust and erotic fascination) forces him to develop a new strategy for introducing a bodily dimension into the seemingly rational designs of Constructivism, and to allow for a different type of dialog between subject and object, i.e., something that provides, gives space to, even encourages an erotic investment in objects, while not giving in to fetishism. In this sense, we should not understand these developments as merely a *negation* of subjectivity, corporeality, desire, etc., but as a way to *rethink* such notions on the basis of a new assemblage of man and technology that allows desire to circulate in a different way.

Now, cross-reading the Soviet vision of the socialist object with the strategies for creating a new type of consumer subject in the emerging welfare state provides us with a way to understand the logic of desire that is operative in both of these attempts, and whose ramifications undoubtedly ought to be examined in other versions of the European avant-garde. This issue was never just to control, discipline, and mould a subject from the outside, although this dimension is there, too, but to always also do so on the basis of a more complex assessment of the resources for this project in the subject itself. The bureaucratic and organizational *eros* need not be unequivocally opposed to the realization of freedom, but should instead be understood as a project to establish a link between the "individual" and the "collective" part of the psyche,

27 Christina Kiaer provides a psychoanalytically oriented account of this particular work in "Rodchenko in Paris," *October* 75, winter 1996, pp. 3-35.

which in its turn was understood to engender not only a passive acceptance on the part of the subject, but an active response that would transform the way we deal with things on the everyday level.

The differences between the utopian dimension of Constructivism and the much more down-to-earth pragmatism of the emerging welfare state should obviously not be erased, and it is true that the actual outcome of these projects would differ enormously. The welfare state version was to a much larger extent capable of providing room for individual variations, and in fact its project was to a large extent precisely to perform this task while still retaining control over the entire cycle of production and consumption at an overarching level. The idea of a socialist object was never realized, and to the extent that the concepts proposed by Arvatov survived at all, they did so in a terrifyingly repressive rhetoric of the New Man that would emerge out of state-controlled socialism, where the level of subjective fantasy was transformed to the level of a post-historical montage that Boris Groys has analyzed in terms of Stalinism as a "total work of art."

My proposal here has been that these two techniques for producing a modern subject, their differences notwithstanding, communicate over the vast cultural and ideological chasms that separate them, and that they in fact would continue to inform, albeit in a subterranean fashion, large parts of modernist architectural theory for a long time to come. A more detailed analysis of the structure of desire in early modernism remains to be done, but also of it how it would be transformed in a different material culture in the postwar period, where the techniques for the production of subjects and objects as "images" would achieve a wholly new level of efficiency, and where the unconscious levels were mobilized in a much more explicit fashion, to the extent that psychoanalysis itself could become a technique for achieving this within a far more encompassing "organizational complex."[28] This development does, however, not break in any clear-cut fashion with the pre-war conceptions, and we should be wary of understanding it in terms of a "postmodern" break with a "modernism" understood as predicated exclusively on a simplistic idea of function. There were always essential aspects of subjectivity and desire implied in the idea of function, just as the idea of desire could contain strong organizational *eros.*

28 For the definition of this term, see Reinhold Martin: *The Organizational Complex: Architecture, Media, and Corporate Space,* Cambridge, Mass.: MIT, 2003.

About the author

Sven-Olov Wallenstein teaches philosophy and esthetics at Södertörn University in Stockholm, and is editor-in-chief of the magazine Site. He is the translator of many philosophical works (Kant, Hegel, Husserl, Foucault, and many others), as well as the author of numerous books, including: *Essays, Lectures* (2007), *The Silences of Mies* (2008), and *Biopolitics and the Emergence of Modern Architecture* (2009). He is currently completing a book on Hegel's phenomenology and a co-edited volume with essays on Swedish Modernism, entitled *Architecture, Consumption, and the Welfare State.*

FINLAND WONDERLAND

ALVAR AALTO AND FINLAND'S GEOPOLITICAL DILEMMA

Eeva-Liisa Pelkonen

Perhaps more than any other modern architect, Alvar Aalto's work and persona have been linked to and explained by his country of origin, Finland. An aerial view of a Finnish lake landscape juxtaposed with an image of the Savoy vase (1937) and the Finnish Pavilion at the 1939/40 *New York World's Fair* in the second edition of Sigfried Giedion's influential *Space, Time and Architecture: The Growth of a New Tradition* in 1949 presented a shorthand argument by suggesting that the essence of Finland flows, as if naturally, into Aalto's architectural forms. Although the geography of Aalto's architecture has acquired new readings, the idea of Aalto being a unique and quintessentially Finnish architect still dominates.

Giedion's ambiguous statement, "Finland is with Aalto wherever he goes,"[1] is, however, still worth citing, as it implies that this emphasis developed in tandem with Aalto's engagement with the world at large. Indeed, Aalto traveled extensively and had a lot to say about Finnish architecture, its relationship to international influence, as well as about Finland's geopolitical situation. While certainly not representative of the mainstream of Finnish architecture of his time, Aalto was very preoccupied with Finland's cultural, political and economic future, believing that his words and works could help shape the country's destiny. Finland and Finnish culture was a major theme of Aalto's writings from early on. "Finnish Homes" (1922), "Landscape in Central Finland" (1925), "Letter from Finland" (1931), "Finland" (1940), "Finland as a Model for World Development" (1949), and "Finland Wonderland" (1950) are just few of his article and book titles. The word "geography" appears in the title of one of the key texts dealing with the relationship between architecture and geography, namely, "The Geography of the Housing Question" from 1932.

Aalto's writings and library reveal a parallel between his preoccupation with various geographic and geopolitical narratives and the historical events that marked the most volatile period in Finnish history, from the Declaration of Independence through the Cold War. There is no doubt that Aalto's life and career were affected by these tumultuous events. A letter written to Frank Lloyd Wright during the Finno-Russian Winter

1 Sigfried Giedion: *Space, Time and Architecture: the Growth of a New Tradition,* Cambridge: Harvard University Press, 1949 [1941], p. 567. German translation: *Raum, Zeit, Architektur. Die Entstehung einer neuen Tradition,* Basel: Birkhäuser, 2007.

War in January 1940 is emblematic both of Aalto's engagement as well as his ability to tailor the words to his audience:

> The Russian attack on Finland was more directed against a social development which proved superior to the practically unproven doctrines of [the] Soviets than by geographical or territorial motives. Because of that the front in Finland is not a national front nor a front of socialism against bourgeoisie but the front no. 1 of the west – the front where the unsuccessful theory overpowered by tsaristic [sic] methods stands on one side and a balanced Western social development with a bright future it stands on the other side.[2]

An article entitled "Finland" published in *Architectural Forum* the same year mapped the foundation of Finnish modernism on the lines of American regionalism.

> Even though there is today in Finland, as in all countries, a good deal of superficial modernism, the country itself, its climate, resources, topography and ways of living afford a mass of material which forms a good base for the solution of problems of contemporary architecture.[3]

The "Finland" article was aimed at convincing his American audience that the Finns had nothing to do with the (putatively) Communist-infested international modern movement. As in the letter to Wright, Aalto avoided using words like *national*, or any language that might suggest that Finland was motivated by a nationalist agenda.

To be sure, Aalto was well-versed in statecraft and saw writings and architecture as a means to promote and even act out various geographical scripts. His geographic narratives produced terminology, representations, and spatial products whose goal was to understand and reinforce national culture, on one hand, and conceptualize relationships to other countries, on the other.

2 Letter to Frank Lloyd Wright, 8 January 1940; AAA document.

3 Alvar Aalto: "Finland," in: *Architectural Forum,* June 1940, p. 399.

Significantly, Aalto did not reject architecture's ties to geographic locations at different historical moments. In the immediate aftermath of the Declaration of Independence, he used the word *national* architecture to reinforce the uniqueness of Finnish culture. The country was seen as a distinct entity with its own architectural sensibility, even when subject to external influences. At this point he was interested in various stylistic motifs and their local variations. The idea of *international* influence developed in the late 1920s, specifically through an interest in the international modern movement, as Aalto became more and more aware that a nation was not an island but existed in reciprocal relationships with other countries. At this time he started to associate internationalism with a spatial product that today we would call a network – a system of linkages and exchanges with many nodes. At the same time, around the mid-1920s, Aalto became exposed to the pan-European movement and started to emphasize mobility across, and even the dissolution of, national boundaries. This provoked further interest in dynamism and mobility. Contact with American regionalists during late-1930s and 1940s and helped him to take a pragmatist approach to geographic questions emphasizing management of economic, human, and natural resources during the period of postwar Finnish reconstruction, which laid the foundation for the future economic prosperity of the country. The spatial idea behind *regionalism* was a nested network, in which the country's internal infrastructural, settlement, and production networks are supported by and connected to the larger global networks of international commerce.

After the Second World War, as Aalto became a self-described *universalist* and *humanist*, he started to invest his architecture with formal and semantic ambiguity. This, I will argue, correlated with Finland's attempt to avoid being drawn into further international conflicts by becoming a neutral country. Considering Aalto's deep engagement with his country's fate, especially during the Second World War, it comes as a surprise that during the late 1940s and early 1950s he often talked about the creative potential within the human psyche and in the process mystified his own design approach. In the much quoted article "Architettura e arte concreta" (Architecture and concrete art), commissioned in 1947 by another Italian friend, Ernesto Rogers, for the Italian magazine *Domus* and later published as "The Trout and the Stream," Aalto declared himself a "practicing artist," describing his design process as follows:

> This is what I do – sometimes quite instinctively – in such a case. I forget the whole maze of problems for a while, as soon as the feel of the assignment and the innumerable demands it involves have sunk into my subconscious. I then move on to a method of working that is very much like abstract art. I simply draw by instinct, not architectural syntheses, but what are sometimes quite childlike compositions, and in this way, on an abstract basis, the main idea gradually takes shape, a kind of universal substance that helps me to bring the numerous contradictory components in harmony.[4]

At first, Aalto's statement appears to suggest that art is a way to escape reality; he talks about the "burden" of architects having to deal with "social, humanitarian, economic, and technological requirements combined with psychological problems affecting both the individual and the group."[5] Yet within a postwar context informed by existentialism and phenomenology, Aalto's statements are apt: the revolution was expected to happen from within an individual and national psyche. Neither was Aalto's interest in this quasi-intuitive design method and architectural experience devoid of geopolitical content. His quest for "freedom" of formal production and an open-ended, poetic richness of meaning was homologous with the social and political freedom he associated with Western democratic societies at the time.

Yet, freedom as well as the possibility of self-realization from within was, to say the least, a relative term in Finland during the 1950s and 1960s. The question of how to manage relations with the Soviet Union had dominated Finnish interior and foreign policy from its inception. Soviet influence intensified when postwar Europe was being divided into two territorial blocs. Urho Kekkonen (1900-1986), Finland's president from 1956 to 1982, was masterful at dealing with the Soviets, cunningly maintaining Finland's delicate autonomy year after year.

The idea of Finland being a harbinger of a new, presumably free, world preoccupied Aalto from the late 1940s onwards. Not only did he start to make frequent claims that

4 Aalto: "Architettura e arte concreta," in: *Domus,* no. 225, Milano, 1947, p. 108; English translation in Göran Schildt: *Alvar Aalto in His Own Words,* New York: Rizzoli, p. 108.

5 Ibid.

Finland was a western democratic country at this point, but also that freedom and democratic values could become the defining factors in Finland's political and social life, as well as its calling card to the outside world. The 1949 article "Finland as a Model for World Development" put forward a simple recipe: following the logic of nature and its self-generative process will lead to architecture that is equally free. Free architecture will subsequently promote freedom in human society.

> Nature is a symbol of freedom. Sometimes it is actually the source of the concept of freedom, and its maintainer. By basing our technical master plans firmly on nature, we have every chance of turning the tide, making our daily work and all its forms increase freedom, rather than reduce it.[6]

Aalto intensified his calls for freedom a year after Finland and the Soviet Union signed the Treaty of Friendship, Cooperation and Mutual Assistance in 1948, which ended a four-year period of uncertainty about whether Finland would become part of the Eastern Bloc. The events following World War Two, however, had long-term consequences for Finland's future that were caused by unanticipated geopolitical shifts. When America's former ally, the Soviet Union, became its ideological enemy, Europe became divided into West and East. Finland was no longer considered the far-end corner of Europe, but instead a country caught in the middle of Cold War intrigues and tensions. As a consequence, while never becoming part of the Eastern Bloc per se, Finland stayed under the Soviet political influence for decades to come.

We have seen how regionalism went hand in hand with the attempt to restructure the Finnish political affinities towards America in the years during the war. The model, however, proved inadequate in addressing the particularly European – and Finnish – need to reinvent its political and cultural identity in the long term. Aalto's reassessment of Finland's cultural and political affinities reflected on a wider shift towards how Europeans started to position themselves *vis a vis* the new superpowers, the USA and the Soviet Union. Aalto's shift of strategy from an interest in large scale planning to the

6 "Finland as a Model for World Development," in: *Suomalainen Suomi,* no. 5, 1949, p. 1; English translation in Göran Schildt: *Alvar Aalto in His Own Words,* p. 171.

celebration of the ineffable qualities of architecture can be linked to the fact that he was, at the time, growing increasingly skeptical about the ever more powerful country across the Atlantic. Writing to Aino during a teaching engagement at MIT in 1945, Aalto paraphrased Frank Lloyd Wright:

> My America no longer exists [...] Democracy has yielded; various fascisms and such have given us a worldwide monocracy. America has become much more imperialistic than in our days, and so self-sufficient that the civilized people who matter so much to us are no longer as important as they used to be."[7]

While once eager to learn American techniques of prefabrication, he now started to see America as the land of rationalization gone haywire, where people did not know how to live nor feel. Although Aalto never directly criticized the Soviet Union after the war, his ideas about freedom put forward in his writings from the late 1940s and 1950s reflected these new geopolitical realities of the Cold War: the western "free world" against totalitarianism on one hand, and soft European versus hard American values on the other.

Aalto's rejection of America reflects the emergence of the wider European sentiment that, despite their indebtedness to Marshall Plan aid and American military intervention in the war, Europe should not model its future on America. His ideas about architecture and its social role were in many ways reflective of this more general thinking about the future of Europe. As historian Tony Judt has noted, there was increasing consensus that Europe had to go beyond the idea that the continent was simply a "geographic expression,"[8] that is, an amalgamation of distinct nations each with its own autonomous territory.

7 Letter to Aino Aalto, 15 December 1945, quoted in Göran Schildt: *Alvar Aalto: The Mature Years,* New York: Rizzoli, 1991, p. 103.

8 Tony Judt: *Postwar: A History of Europe since 1945,* New York: Penguin, 2005, p. 8.

The idea of Europe that started to emerge after the war – of the continent as an increasingly unified social and political entity – was based on socially progressive ideals that would later make the continent, in the words of Judt, both a "role-model and magnet for individuals and countries alike."[9]

Aalto actively participated in the creation of Finland as a harbinger of these new values during the postwar years. One of his main contributions as a Chairman of the Association of Finnish Architecture was to help found the Museum of Finnish Architecture in 1956, whose main function was to export Finnish architecture abroad. The first in the series of *Finland Builds* exhibitions was opened in London the following year.[10] It portrayed a country with a high standard of living facilitated by quality architecture built in harmony with nature. Aalto, who before the war had been considered first and foremost a Finnish architect, was now declared "one of the most important European men" when he arrived at the opening of the London installation in 1957.[11] Aalto becomes a new standard bearer at this point, with commissions flowing in from different parts of the world.

Italy and Germany both struggling to overcome their fascist past, became particularly fertile ground for Aalto's architectural ideas and their political and cultural subtext. Although Aalto was able to realize only one building in Italy, the Riola Church (1966-67), he won many more commissions and had a wide following among the left-leaning intellectual elite, who saw in Aalto's vision of Finland a hope for a gentler architecture and a self generated culture.

In Germany – which was not only recovering from massive physical destruction after the war, but, due to its apportionment, was literally defined by the division between

9 Ibid.

10 See Petra Ceferin: *Constructing a Legend: The International Exhibitions of Finnish Architecture 1957–1967*, Helsinki: Suomalaisen Kirjallisuuden Seura, 2003; for further discussion of the traveling exhibitions that cemented the reputation of Finnish architecture, Hildi Hawkins has written on the export of Finnish design in "Finding a Place in a New World Order: Finland, America, and the 'Design in Scandinavia' Exhibition of 1954-57," in: Marianne Aav and Nina Stritzler-Levine (eds.): *Finnish Modern Design: Utopian Ideals and Everyday Realities, 1930-1997*, New Haven: Yale University Press, 1998, pp. 232-251.

11 Robert Wraight: "One of the Great Men of Europe Comes to London," in: *Sunday Times*, 14 April 1957, facsimile reprint in Petra Ceferin: "In Pursuit of Finnishness: The Foreign Press on Finnish Architecture, 1957-1967," in: *Arkkitehti*, no. 1, 2004, p. 22.

East and West – the celebration of pure, uninhibited creativity meshed with complex existential and political themes. At the Darmstädter Gespräche (Darmstadt Discussions) in 1951, where Martin Heidegger gave his famous speech "Building, Dwelling, Thinking," the leading German architect-theorist Rudolf Schwarz (1897-1961) put forth ideas about the genesis and experience of form that resonated with Aalto's. Schwarz talked about his "astonishment and wonder [at] how the world exists only in forms, of which each form speaks the truth and does so in an irreplaceable way only to the eye."[12] Schwarz was explicit about why an architect should, at that particular historical moment, start making willful scribbles on paper: he considered it nothing less than a historical responsibility. The open-ended approach to design endorsed an open future. He spoke of the "unplannable" and called for the architect "not [to] overburden himself or the earth with the attempt to eliminate confusion, because the earth and the world require confusion ... He must allow space for confusion, enormous free space."[13] Aalto was admired by a group of German architects, including Schwarz, who aimed to steer German postwar architecture away from what they started to consider, somewhat reductively, the rigid Bauhaus legacy, toward a more heterogeneous spatial and formal expression able to trigger deep existential reflection. Not surprisingly, Aalto's Villa Mairea (1937-39) was included in an exhibition of exemplary buildings that took place in tandem with the Darmstadt Conversations. By its completion year, 1939, Germany had attacked Poland and World War Two had begun. In retrospect, the building was a swansong of all the progressive ideals of the modern movement.

12 Rudolf Schwarz: "Das Anliegen der Baukunst," in: Otto Bartning in cooperation with Magistrat der Stadt Darmstadt, Komitee Darmstädter Gespräch 1951 (ed.): *Mensch und Raum,* Darmstadt: Neue Darmstädter Verlagsanstalt, 1952, pp. 60-71, 60. English translation in Lynnette Widder: "The 'Darmstadt Conversation': On the Reconstruction of Meaning and the Construction of Dwelling," paper presented at the conference "Architecture and Art: New Visions, New Strategies," 2nd International Alvar Aalto Research Conference on Modern Architecture, August 12-14, Jyväskylä, Finland; reprint in conference proceedings, Helsinki: Alvar Aalto Academy, 2005, p. 133. My discussion on Schwarz is greatly indebted to Widder's illuminating paper.

13 Rudolf Schwarz: "Das Unplanbare," in: *Baukunst und Werkform* 1947/48, reprint in Ulrich Conrads (ed.): *Die Städte himmeloffen: Reden und Reflexionen über den Wiederaufbau des Untergegangenen und die Wiederkehr des Neuen Bauens 1948-49,* ausgewählt aus den ersten beiden Ausgaben der Vierteljahreshefte *Baukunst und Werkform,* Berlin: Birkhäuser, 2003, pp. 97-99; English translation in Lynnette Widder: "The 'Darmstadt Conversation,'" p. 134.

Considering the complex political factors and the heavy burden of history, it perhaps comes as no surprise that Germany, faced with the task of reinventing its culture, singled out Aalto as its architect of choice for three significant housing and public projects. The most emblematic of these projects was the Hansaviertel housing block (1955-57), commissioned by the City of West Berlin in response to massive housing developments built along the Stalinallee in Soviet East Berlin. The area contained buildings by the world's leading architects, including Le Corbusier, Gropius, and Oscar Niemeyer, all based upon existing modern mass-housing typologies – the slab and the tower in a park-like setting.[14] Aalto's strategy was to envision a new typology for a housing block by designing two low towers consisting of quasi-independent courtyard houses. By emphasizing the individuality of each unit, he provided a potent symbol of democratic, anti-Soviet collectivism, while the grouping of these units was communal enough to avoid any reference to extreme individualism. The covered area between the two towers was a perfect metaphor for all new boundaries that had been drawn in Europe, at times separating families and countrymen from each other. The plan of the Essen Opera House (competition 1959, built posthumously between 1981 and 1988), was, on the other hand, a fitting example of the opposite: a space becoming a kind of "universal substance" without boundaries, in which a "heap," to use Schwarz's term, of different programmatic zones melt inside a continuous skin. Aalto had described just such an approach in the *Domus* article, as had his German colleague, with his conception of "confused" or "free" space.

Aalto contributed to the era's oblique architectural discourse by emphasizing the impact buildings had on people. In a 1955 lecture, "Between Humanism and Materialism," given in Vienna, he talked about his desire to go beyond mere "humanizing" and consider the visual and symbolic impact of buildings.

> "I should perhaps devote the last few words of my talk," he said, "to the formal aspects of architecture. Although the solving of architectural problems is a necessary

14 For further discussion of the politics behind the Hansaviertel, see Francesca Rogier: "The Monumentality of Rhetoric: The Will to Rebuild in Postwar Berlin," in: Sarah Williams Goldhagen and Réjean Legault (eds.): *Anxious Modernisms: Experimentation in Postwar Architectural Culture,* Montréal: Canadian Centre for Architecture, 2000, pp. 165-189.

humanizing procedure, the old question regarding form and monumentality remains a reality that architects must still confront, as they have always had to do."[15]

Significantly, the speech was published in *Der Bau* magazine in Austria, and then in the German magazine *Baukunst-Werkbund*, whose editorial board included Rudolf Schwarz.

It is interesting to consider the relationship between architecture and politics, and, subsequently speculate about architecture as power, from this perspective. Emphasis on form was a means to transcend actual conditions and contingencies and it is exactly the ambiguity of meaning so created that reflected Finland's political goals: to transcend Russia's political influence and become, at least in people's imaginations, a politically ambiguous neutral zone, with no ideological attributes. We could thus draw two conclusions about the political dimension of Aalto and his architecture. On one hand, his quasi-existential, open-ended design method of the postwar years reflected the Finnish Cold War political atmosphere, which was marked by its own share of conceit, ambiguity, and double-play. One the other hand, the emphasis on form and for not settling to make architecture reflect helped shape, formulate, and imagine a new Finland.

Aalto's international reception was also tied to Finland's geopolitical dilemma. The renewed interest in Aalto during the late 1970s by a new generation of scholars like Kenneth Frampton (*1930) and Colin St. John Wilson (1922-2007) can be viewed against the political backdrop of the end of the Cold War, which officially took place at the 1975 European Security Conference Summit in Helsinki. Initiated by President Kekkonen, the event also marked Finland's emergence as an officially neutral country able to transcend political conflicts between East and West. As if knowing that he had brought his geopolitical narrative to full conclusion, Aalto died a year later. Appropriately, the summit took place in Aalto's Finlandia House, one of his last designs, which consisted of a concert hall, finished in 1971, and a Congress wing, completed in 1975 for the meeting of heads of state. The building can be understood as an open-ended

15 Aalto: "Between Humanism and Materialism" (Zwischen Humanismus und Materialismus), in: Der Bau, no.7/8, 1955, pp. 174-175, reprint in *Baukunst und Werkform,* vol. 6, 1956, pp. 298-300; English translation from Schildt: *Alvar Aalto in His Own Words,* p. 179.

field of meaning and a perfect emblem of Finland's newly gained geopolitical status. References to classical language abounded – the amphitheater-shaped auditorium, the fluted columns – yet it was hard to pinpoint either the geographic or temporal origins of the building; the quasi-naturalistic zigzagging glass wall in the conference wing made a generic allusion to nature; and the white walls served as a perfect metaphor for neutrality as an emblem of freedom, making a case for a freedom from geopolitical constrains.

So if we were to ask how central Finland is to the understanding of Aalto's work, the answer would be that Finland's political and economic situation during its existence has been precarious and fragile, always mutable, with wide ranging implications for Aalto's life, career, and reception. Aalto can be credited for his vision of a better, worldlier future for Finland and his energetic work toward that dream. We cannot therefore fully understand either Aalto or his work without taking the geographic context into consideration – and vice versa: we cannot fully understand Finland without Aalto.

About the author

Eeva-Liisa Pelkonen is associate professor at Yale School of Architecture. Her scholarly work deals with the genesis and meaning of architectural form in different national and historical contexts. She is currently working on a book and exhibition on Kevin Roche with her students and is the author of: *Achtung Architektur! Image and Phantasm in Contemporary Austrian Architecture* (1996); Eero Saarinen: *Shaping the Future* (co-ed. 2006), and Alvar Aalto: *Architecture, Modernity and Geopolitics* (2009). Her book on Saarinen won the Sir Banister Fletcher Award and the Philip Johnson Award.

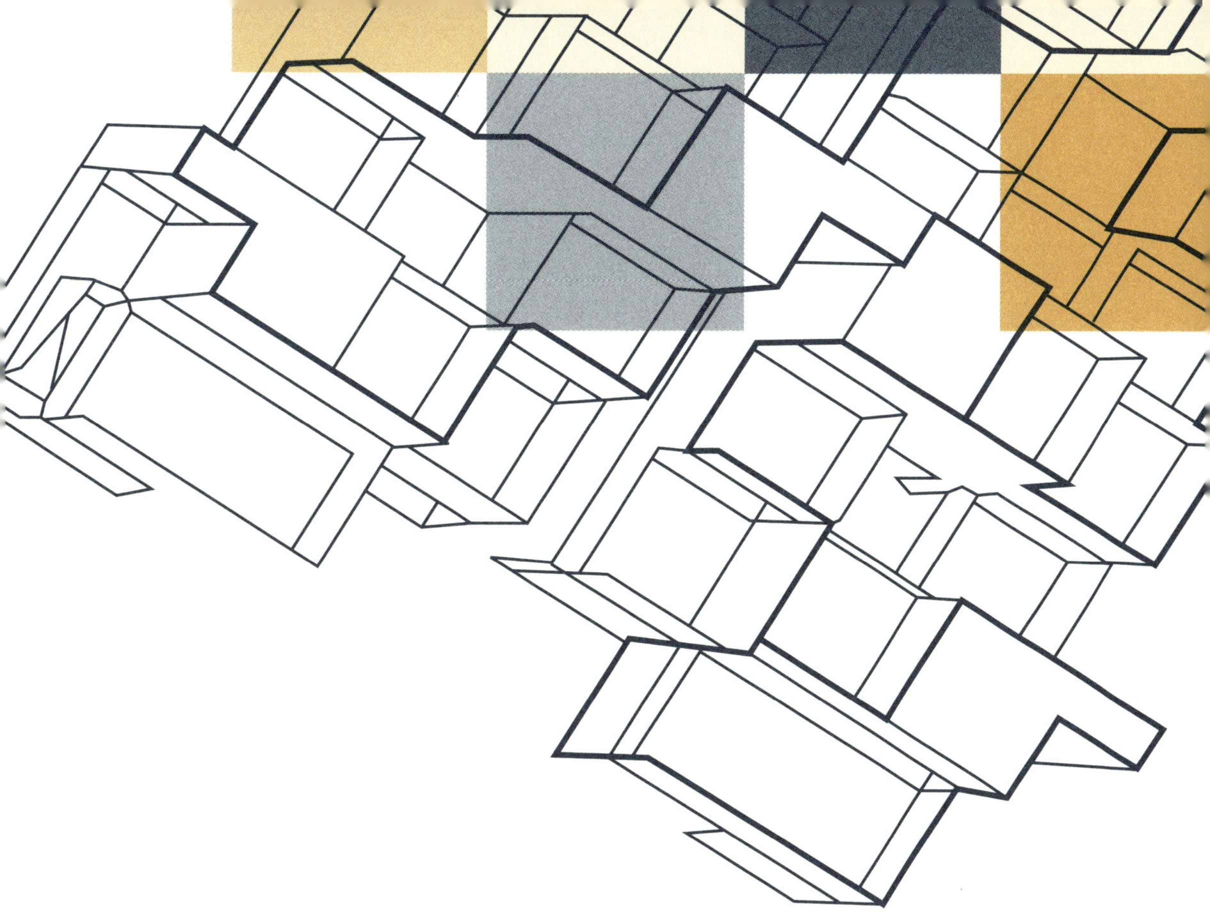

MODIFIED MODERNISM

THE RELATIONAL ARCHITECTURE OF THE LOW-RISE HIGH-DENSITY MOVEMENT

Mari Hvattum

The fiftieth anniversary of the Hansaviertel provides a welcome opportunity to revisit the architectural ideals of the postwar era. A modernist showpiece, the Hansaviertel was built to display the modern and democratic West. It recruited the architectural elite of its day including international hot-shots such as Le Corbusier, Walter Gropius, and Oscar Niemeyer. The grand experiment in the Tiergarten, however, exhibited a marked slant towards the Nordic, with contributions by well-established names such as Alvar Aalto and Arne Jacobsen. So significant was this contribution that today, fifty years later, seminars are arranged on the Nordic contribution to German post-war architecture; a cultural migration informed more by politics than esthetics, yet nevertheless producing a distinct architectural expression. The Nordic welfare state provided a promising model for social reconstruction after the Second World War, and the Hansaviertel was its embodiment. Despite the Nordic slant, no Norwegian architects contributed to the Hansaviertel. Their absence speaks of several factors. First of all, there simply were no Norwegian architects of international prominence similar to Aalto or Jacobsen. Surprisingly, many of the talented Norwegian modernists from the 1930s had died young, either from disease or war service (Lars Backer, Ove Bang, Fritjof Reppen, to mention but a few), and the ones left had been quickly absorbed into postwar reconstruction, an undertaking geared more to infrastructure and planning than to the production of architectural masterpieces. In the early 1950s, however, a generation of young Norwegian architects emerged with the ambition to modify and transform the modernist agenda into a distinctly social democratic form

of architecture. If the Nordic welfare state adopted the non-hierarchical as its most characteristic feature and its most sought-after ideal, then these architects sought its architectural counterpart: a non-hierarchical architecture. In fact, when Bernhard Tschumi yearned for the non-hierarchical in his 1980s project for Parc de la Villette, he was echoing a concern that already had a long history in postwar architectural discourse.[1] In this essay, I will scrutinize the so-called Low-Rise High-Density movement

1 As Bernard Tschumi writes: "[...] the Parc de la Villette project had a specific aim: to prove that it was possible to construct a complex architectural organisation without resorting to traditional rules of composition, hierarchy, and order." "Parc de la Villette, Paris," in: Papadakis, Andreas; Catherine Cooke and Andrew Benjamin (eds.): *Deconstruction. Omnibus Volume,* London: Academy Editions, 1989, pp. 175-181, pp. 177-178.

in Norway in first decades after the Second World War, paying particular attention to the ways in which the modernist agenda was being modified in this period.

The Failure of the New

As the modernist doctrines went from being utopian manifestos to constituent premises for postwar reconstruction, their content came under critical scrutiny. Functionalism's reductivist approach to the individual as well as to the city became the subject of increasing disapproval – provoking headlines such as "The Failure of the New Towns" and "Outrage!"[2] It was a criticism that took many guises. On the one hand, Gordon Cullen and the Townscape Movement – with *The Architectural Review* as a faithful mouthpiece – called for a return to a lost *Gemeinschaft* and the re-conquest of the traditional townscape's visual qualities. On the other hand, a far more progressivist critique was voiced from within CIAM itself; a critique which would eventually lead to the whole organisation dissolving into several competing factions. By far the most important of these was Team X, whose Doorn-manifesto from 1954 challenged the very principles of orthodox modernism: "...Urbanism considered and developed in the terms of the Charte d'Athene tends to produce 'towns' in which vital human associations are inadequately expressed."[3] Unlike the Townscape movement, Team 10 did not promote the return to a lost Gemeinschaft. Instead, they sought to redefine prewar modernism for a postwar era, bringing modernism up to date, so to speak. Key to this redefinition was the attention to relations: to "vital human associations," as the Doorn manifesto put it. The static and atomized four-zone principle of the Athens Charter seemed hopelessly inadequate in a world in which demographic, economic, political, and cultural conditions were undergoing rapid and radical change. As Peter and Alison Smithson proclaimed at the 10th CIAM congress in Dubrovnik in 1956:

2 Headlines of *Architectural Review*, no. 7, 1953 and no. 15, 1955.

3 Peter Smithson: "Statement on Habitat," Doorn, January 1954, in: Alison Smithson (ed.): *The Emergence of Team 10 out of CIAM*, London: Architectural Association, Graduate School, 1982, p. 29 and 33.

> The new aim is an active environment, and the technique to realise it that of urban dynamics ... It is concerned with developing a community structure that can change, yet be comprehensible at each stage of development. A structure based on human associations, how people come together (Cluster), how they move (Mobility) and on the relationship between the parts and the whole (Growth and Change).[4]

The Smithsons' competition project for Berlin from 1957 (roughly simultaneous with the inauguration of the Hansaviertel, as it happens) bears out this focus on dynamic change. Preserving Berlin's iron grid structure, they overlaid the existing grid with a complex structure of elevated walkways. The proposal introduced few buildings in a traditional sense, but rather a series of hubs capable of absorbing various programmatic requirements as well as of connecting the different levels of infrastructure in a complex, web-like structure. In marked contrast to Corbusier's tabula rasa plans where monumental towers are set in green and splendid isolation, the Smithsons' Hauptstadt Berlin heralds an architecture in which the body of the building is subordinated to the overall structure and in which the structure itself embraces multiple layers of history and use. The structuralist undertone of the Smithsons' approach is very noticeable. The Team 10 generation of architects had read their Levi-Strauss; some had probably even read their Saussure, and were certainly familiar with system theorists like Norbert Wiener. And just like Saussure proclaimed that language has to do with the relationships of sounds rather than words, the architect-structuralists envisioned an architecture of relations rather than buildings. The radical proposition of this generation architects was thus to envision an architecture in which the architectural object itself is devoid of significance, where buildings are subsumed into a dynamic, self-regulating structure capable of changing and growing.

4 Peter and Alison Smithson: "The tenth congress of CIAM, Dubrovnik, August 1956," in: Smithson (ed.): *The Emergence of Team 10,* p. 71.

The Team 10 generation yearned for a relational architecture. They wanted to "come closer to the shifting centre of human reality and build its counterform," as Aldo van Eyck put it.[5] And yet, the resulting architecture was often rather daunting – megastructures as monumental and willful as the modernism they were trying to revise. Byker Wall, Robin Hood Gardens, or Habitat '67 in Montreal, are examples of projects that, while relational in conception, are pretty monumental in scale. A less ostentatious interpretation of the relational ideal can be found in the fiercely anti-esthetic architecture of the Nordic welfare state. In Norway, such ideals developed not least through the framework of the so-called PAGON group, established in the late forties on the initiative of Christian Norberg-Schulz. Norberg-Schulz had come back to Norway from Zurich in 1949, bringing his teacher Sigfried Giedion, with him, in person as well as in spirit. Intent on establishing a Norwegian chapter of CIAM, Norberg-Schulz gathered a group of young architects, most of whom had attended the so-called architects crisis-course immediately after the war. A sort of improvised education for students who had had their architectural education interrupted by the war, the "crisis course" was taught by Arne Korsmo and included students like Sverre Fehn, Geir Grung, Odd Østbye, and Håkon Mjelva. Jørn Utzon – a close friend of Korsmo – was a sort of honorary guest in the group. In 1950, PAGON (Progressive Arkitekters Gruppe Oslo Norge) was formed, with Norberg-Schulz and Korsmo as its leading figures.[6]

Reports from the CIAM conferences throughout the 1950s reveal the active participation of the PAGON group. In the 1955 CIAM meeting, for instance, Grung and Korsmo are reported to have presented "A flexible Housing Group; a study of the relation between buildings, their growth, and landscape." No illustrations are provided, but perhaps the mentioned project is the same as the one presented a few years earlier

5 Quoted in: Alison Smithson (ed.): *Team 10 Primer.* London/ Cambridge, Mass.: MIT Press, 1968, p. 43.

6 For a brief history of PAGON and its development, see Elisabeth Tostrup and Nina Berre: "Pagon og modernismens reformulering," in: *Byggekunst,* no. 5, 2006, pp. 24-26.

in the PAGON issue of *Byggekunst* from 1952.[7] Showing low, informally grouped clusters of small housing units, the scheme recalls Utzon's low and dense Kingo houses, built some years later. The composition was decidedly un-monumental, its meandering structure and modular units allowing no hierarchical differentiation – no "high" or "low", "up" or "down", "central" or "peripheral". As the CIAM report notes, the project is carefully adjusted to the landscape, focusing on relationships – between landscape and buildings as well as between the individual units – rather than on the buildings themselves.

The 1952 PAGON issue is interesting in many respects, not least for its early and incisive critique of the welfare state as it was about to develop in the Nordic countries. As the unsigned editorial proclaims:

> [...] instead of developing a free and stimulating co-existence between all people, on an equal economic basis [...] the struggle for material conditions has brought on the most comprehensive petit-bourgeois attitude ever encountered in history.[8]

The pursuit of a secure and fair economic basis had just about succeeded, the author proposed, but the result of this new-found wealth was depressing: social conformity and materialism seemed to prevail. A disgusting "coziness" (the author(s) actually used the English term) had come to dominate the architectural scene, threatening the clarity of the whole modern project to which PAGON remained firmly wedded.

While defending modernism against postwar cravings for the cozy and the luxurious, PAGON was at the same time highly critical of the outcome of modernist planning. The satellite towns, in particular, were at the receiving end; their soulless environments were seen as the product of a static, paternalistic and reductive social vision. The satellite towns were criticized as impoverished and alienating, a shortcom-

7 Unsigned article "Bolig?," in: *Byggekunst,* no. 6/7, 1952, pp. 108-109.

8 "[...] istedenfor å å utvikle et fritt og stimulerende samliv mellom alle mennesker, på noenlunde samme økonomiske basis, noe vi beginner å få, har kampen for de materielle vilkår ført oss inn i historiens mest gjennomgripende småborgerlighet." unsigned editorial, in: Ibid., p. 93, my translation.

ing caused by CIAM's narrowly scientific criteria and its reductivist focus on physical and functional aspects over the social and psychological. As the editorial sarcastically remarks, "What does it matter if you save the housewife for two steps, if she has got divorced in the meantime?"[9] The welfare state had become,

> [...] a giant fridge in which people are condemned to opulence. [...] A society of well fed and handsome guinea pigs, awaiting – yes, it is difficult to say which – progress. They live in a mechanized and chromed world, where each man receives his destiny like a railway ticket, and where every independent thought represents a pathological case.[10]

The vehemence of the diagnosis is in many ways surprising. After all, the Norway of 1952 had hardly witnessed very many crass examples of soul-destroying satellite towns. The few that had been built – Lambertseter outside Oslo, most notably – had been received with popular acclaim and celebrated as the victorious advent of modernity in Norway. Yet for the PAGON group, drawing on international debate as much as on local experience, the satellite town represented a principle that seemed outdated even before it was realized. Based on the static principle of zoning, it was an urban form incapable of adapting to the rapid changes in postwar society. Furthermore, the mass-produced and standardized dwellings were both causes of and contributors to the dreaded social conformity, which was turning modern man into a well fed guinea pig in a giant social experiment.

The solution to the guinea pig problem was for PAGON, as it was for Team X, an architecture of flexibility and adaptability; an architecture that would make it possible for the individual to shape and change his or her own environment. The didactically arranged photographs of the PAGON issue illustrate such participation with a clarity

---

9 Ibid.

10 The anonymous author here quotes what an equally anonymous "obnoxious French voice" (Le Corbusier?) is reputed to have said about Sweden: "Sverige – et kjempekjøleskap hvor mennesker er dømt til vellevned [...]. Et samfunn av velgjødde og prektige eksperimentmarsvin som venter på – ja det er vanskelig å si – hvilke fremskritt – De lever i en mekanisk og forniklet verden, hvor alle mottar sin skjebne som en jernbanebillet og hvor enhver selvstendig tanke utgjør et patologisk innslag," "Bolig?" in: Ibid., p. 109, my translation.

bordering on caricature. One image carries the intriguing title "The family collaborating to dwell" and shows an impeccably dressed family – mother, father, and child – building a model of what we must presume is their future home.[11] Dwelling, we are to understand, is a collaborative activity, not a passive subsuming into a standard container. Through examples ranging from traditional Japanese architecture to Jose Lluis Sert's modular facades and Soul Steinberg's acerbic cartoons, the PAGON group promoted a notion of a flexible, adaptable, and unequivocal architecture in which variety within order was cultivated as the principle esthetic ideal. In the same issue, Arne Korsmo presented his highly idiosyncratic version of this ideal under the label "The Mecano of the Home," referring both to the popular modular toy kit and to more esoteric notions of organic order and the lawfulness of growth and change.[12]

Korsmo and Norberg-Schulz would implement the ideals of variety, order, and flexibility in their joint housing project in the hills of Vettakollen, outside Oslo. The three little houses in Planetveien were to embody a new kind of modernism, very different from the monumental white villas of the thirties (to which Korsmo had contributed several magnificent exemplars). Three simple, boxlike volumes set in the wooded slopes, with sparse detailing and an austere geometry, the Planetvei houses are certainly un-monumental. However, behind the minimalist glass and steel façades with their subtle Mies van der Rohe-like modularity, we find a series of rich and varied spaces with great attention to qualities of use. It is particularly Korsmo's own house that is interesting in this respect. Built for himself and his wife, the designer Grete Prytz-Korsmo (later Prytz-Kittelsen), the house is composed of a series of spaces that are all eminently transformable: the living room (unfurnished save its 100 60 x 60 centimeter cushions in different colors) transforms into a stage and lecture hall, the kitchen turns into a workshop, and the upstairs bedrooms with its fold-away beds mutates into an office. Lovingly describing the house as "our working-home", Korsmo

11 Ibid., p. 113.

12 "Hjemmets mekano," in: Ibid., pp. 110-113. The article is unsigned, yet derives undoubtedly from Arne Korsmo, who promoted this concept as, among other things, a teaching tool. For a discussion of Korsmo's somewhat mystifying "Mecano of the home," see Elisabeth Tostrup: "A critical architectural icon and its contextual argumentation," in: Jane Rendell et al.: *Critical Architecture,* London: Routledge, 2007, pp. 269-270.

cherished its adaptability, its lack of architectural pretension, and its capacity to accommodate modern life in all its permutations.[13]

Korsmo's house in Planetveien sums up much of the modified modernism of the 1950s. Its modular construction, un-monumental expression, and functional flexibility made it a paradigmatic example of postwar modernism. In a certain sense, Planetveien encapsulates the most pressing concern and the most difficult dilemma for the postwar welfare state: how to create a non-hierarchical system while at the same time cultivating and creating differences – qualitative, programmatic, and architectural. The political equality promoted by the welfare state was laudable, yet, as this generation of architects saw it, it represented at the same time a real risk of straitjacket homogeneity, stifling individual expression. To allow individual expression within a non-hierarchical system was the challenge taken up by the postwar generation of architects; a challenge clearly expressed in Norwegian 1950s architecture.

PAGON – or "Group 5," as its inner circle would sometimes be called – were fighting a war on three fronts. On the one hand, they battled against the reductive and economically motivated functionalism that had come to dominate postwar reconstruction. On the other, they resisted the willfulness of subjective expression threatening to make late modern architecture just as eclectic as the much hated Historicism of the nineteenth century. In addition, they rebelled against the dreaded "coziness" – the nationalist nostalgia creeping back into Norwegian architecture in the 1950s – with its idyllic cottages and its chequered windows so prevalent in *Byggekunst* in the 1950s. Against these three equally untenable positions, PAGON adopted a distinctly structuralist argument: architecture has to tap into the underlying structures of modern society – social, economical, cultural – and translate them into meaningful form.

PAGON's dismay at the postwar situation was largely concordant with international architectural discourse as it was shaped by CIAM and, after 1958, by Team 10. Modernism had failed to fulfill its most fundamental duty: to be modern. As Oscar Hansen pointed out with great clarity:

13 See Arne Korsmo's presentation of the house in *Byggekunst,* no. 7, 1955, pp. 174-183. Elisabeth Tostrup offers an elucidating reading of Korsmo's house in Planetveien in her "To hus – kontraster på felles grunn," in: *Byggekunst,* no. 2, 2002, pp. 48-55.

Which are the objectives one might raise against Architecture as we know it?

1. It did not solve the problem of number [...]
2. As an expression of closed form contemporary architecture cannot be adapted to change; it becomes often outdated, even before being completed.
3. Present architectural conception does not sufficiently take into account the personality of the inhabitants and is too often inhuman
4. It is wasteful of the financial means at our disposal[14]

In short, modern architecture was no longer modern, because its rigid analytics failed to respond to the fast-changing, fast-growing world of the postwar period. The new focus on flexibility, non-hierarchical structures, anti-monumental compositions, and user-participation – direct or indirect – was part of a strategy to save modern architecture and make it up to date.

Structuring the Home

While the structuralist agenda was shared by a whole generation of architects worldwide, it would take on a particular characteristic in the Nordic countries. Perhaps due to the tradition of the self-build combined with the strong public focus on housing, the structuralist ideals in Norway were translated primarily into housing, particularly the so-called Low-Rise High-Density movement. A project that displays the ambitions and ideals of this movement is that of Skjettenbyen – a community half an hour north of Oslo. Launched as a competition in 1965, the program called for 1,500 housing units, a figure that would be upped to almost 2,000 in the realized project. In density and brief, the project is quite similar to any other satellite town, and yet, in a tacit acknowledgment of the massive criticism targeting postwar suburbia, the program

14 "The open form in architecture: art for the greater number," Oscar Hansen: *Carré bleu*, January 1961, quoted in A. Smithson (ed.): *Team 10 Primer*, p. 45.

called for "reconsideration of common housing types."[15] And reconsideration they got. The Danish architect Niels Ole Lund's first prize project was based on a low and dense structure of atrium-house clusters, completely overturning the high rise slab model so prevalent at the time. Indeed, all the prize-winning projects applied low-rise structures, and their varied mix of public and private spaces echoes authors such as Serge Chermayeff and Christopher Alexander, whose *Community and Privacy* from 1963 had been avidly read by young Norwegian architects.

While Lund received the first prize, he was not left with the commission. The first and second prize winners merged into a team called Skjettenprosjektering AS, involving talented young architects such as Erik Hultberg, the main man behind the second prize project. The low-rise high-density scheme that emerged was based on cutting-edge modular production, in which a complete production system for prefabricated housing units was incorporated into the project. The project became a real "ars combinatoria" of pre-fab modules, making possible thousands of different combinations and allowing the inhabitants unprecedented possibility to change and adapt their own house. In fact, the project came complete with its own residents' manual, explaining everything from construction details to planning law and extolling the virtues of the self-build. It even included a planning application form to ease the residents' dealings with the planning authorities.[16] Skjettenbyen was a giant experiment towards a democratic, flexible, relational and anti-hierarchical architecture, in which the architect provided an efficient if minimal frame for the resident to develop and "fill" with life and beauty. In the spirit of Oscar Hansen's Open Form, the architects provided first and foremost a system – leaving it to the inhabitants to provide the expression.

The experiment at Skjetten did not go entirely as the architects had hoped. The pre-fab factory was never built, and the plug-in of readymade modules remained a dream. In a heart-rending essay written in the late 1970s, Erik Hultberg revisits the

15 *Norske Arkitektkonkurranser*, no. 116, p. 1965.

16 A detailed presentation of the Skjetten project in English is found in Andrew Rabeneck's review "Adaptable Row Houses in Norway," in: *Architectural Design*, no. 10, 1974, pp. 655-659 – an article that more than anything reveals the systems approach to architectural design predominating this period.

area, lamenting how few of the residents have altered their houses at all. The vibrant colors, the purpose-made extensions, the cartwheels, and the flowerpots had failed to materialize, leaving Skjettenbyen with the impoverished feel of a barren system.[17] Despite this disappointment, however, the many large housing competitions towards the end of the 1960s and beginning of the 1970s were all won by projects promoting similar low-rise, flexible housing structures, in which the architectural expression was to be an outcome of the residents' rather than the architects' design.[18] The ideal of participation and adaptability even filtered through to the competition briefs, becoming, towards the end of the 1970s, a matter of publicly promoted and politically correct requirements. The aim was to create a modified modernism – a modernism that was responsive to individual needs yet at the same time uncompromisingly rational, both in economical and social terms. The reality, however, was less univocal. While the architects dreamed of settlements brimming with local initiative and indigenous expression, the postwar suburban dweller seemed less eager to contribute. The result was areas in which the restrained esthetics of late modernism – intended as a framework to be filled rather than a complete work in itself – was left as an abstract and skeletal frame.

The unwillingness on the part of the architects to create form rather than just systems would become increasingly more pronounced throughout the 1960s. Partly, it was propelled by political ideals – a critique of paternalistic planning – and partly it was driven by a deep fascination for systems and systematic production. The relational ideals of the 1950s were upheld, yet the architectural expression would become increasingly more abstract. An extreme example of this reluctance towards form is given by a housing competition from 1971 on the Dyster Eldor area south of Oslo. The team from Skjetten won, while the young architects Jansen & Thorenfeldt came second.[19] Common to both projects is an extremely abstract approach, in which the

17 Erik Hultberg: "Skjetten revisited," in: *Byggekunst 6,* 1979, pp. 404-405, p. 404.

18 For instance the large competition in 1967 at Risvollan outside Trondheim (*Norske Arkitektkonkurranser,* no. 140, 1967), the Tjensvoll competition outside Stavanger from 1968 (*Norske Arkitektkonkurranser,* no. 161, 1968), and the Dyster Eldor competition from 1971 south of Oslo (*Norske Arkitektkonkurranser,* no. 181, 1971).

19 Jan Jansen and Ragnhild and Truls Thorenfeldt.

dwellings themselves are reduced to diagrammatic combinations within a system of modules. The ultimate illustration of the approach is given by Jansen & Thorenfeldt's illustration of a typical housing cluster in their prize-winning project. The drawing shows two roads, a hedge-like scrawl delineating a block, and in the middle of the block the text: "Group of about 50 houses. Plan to be determined by the residents."[20] Firmly abandoning the responsibility of shaping the physical world, these architects see themselves as political facilitators rather than form-givers.

The rather extreme example of the Dyster Eldor competition brings home a more general point regarding the architectural ideals of the low-rise high-density movement. The dream of a relational architecture in which the architectural object is insignificant is not without its problems. Notwithstanding Yona Friedman's alluring open form grids or the Smithsons' fascinatingly abstract structures, buildings tend to have an undeniable, tangible presence and look that is hard to escape. When Norwegian architects abandoned the problem of form in the 1970s, they unwittingly paved the way for a movement which was to dominate architectural discourse and practice in the next decade, namely figurative post-modernism. The semantic silence of postwar modernism, its contempt for form, and its excessive fascination for systems necessarily brought on a yearning for the opposite – the recognizable figure and the meaningful motif. So, just a few years after he had promoted an unadulterated structuralism, Christian Norberg-Schulz would call for the return to the figurative:

> The basic aim of post-modernism is to re-conquer the figurative dimension. [...] The purpose, to put it simply, is to make architecture comprehensible, and thus human, in the real sense of the word.[21]

When Charles Jenks accused modernism of being too abstract and incomprehensible, he accurately targeted not the sculptural white modernism of the 1920s and 1930s but the abstract systems architecture of the 1960s and 1970s. Like Hultberg lamenting

20 *Norske Arkitektkonkurranser,* no. 181, 1979.

21 Christian Norberg-Schulz: "På vei mot en figurativ arkitektur," in: *Byggekunst,* no. 1, 1985, pp. 4-6, p. 5.

the schematic result at Skjetten, the Low-Rise High-Density movement woke up to the realization that their relational architecture had fallen prey to their own critical diagnosis, becoming "outdated even before being completed."

The relational architecture of the Low-Rise High-Density movement ultimately failed. It did so because the inevitable existence of the architectural object – its materiality, its atmosphere, its meaning – was ignored, and because what was left was somehow not significant enough to make a difference. Noting this failure and analyzing its causes is important not least today, when notions of the architect as a political facilitator are emerging yet again. It seems to me that the experiments of the 1950s – from Korsmo and Norberg-Schulz' understated adaptations at Planetveien to the Hansaviertel's subtle modification of modernist ideals – provide an interesting alternative both to the excessively anti-formalist position of the 1960s and 1970s and the extreme formalism of the 1980s. Just like Aalto and Jacobsen in Berlin, Korsmo and the PAGON group challenged the straitjacket of orthodox modernism and looked for an architecture which allowed for difference on both a socio-political and an architectural level. They did so, however, from a vantage point firmly within the boundaries of building, balancing political critique with innovative design in an admirably concrete kind of way. If there is any point in celebrating the fiftieth anniversary of the Hansaviertel, it should be to scrutinize this short-lived and precarious period in which modernism was modified yet still not drained of its significance.

About the author
Mari Hvattum is associate professor at the Oslo School of Architecture and Design in Norway. She trained as an architect at the Norwegian Institute of Technology and as an architectural historian at the University of Cambridge. She has taught architectural history and theory at several universities in the UK and abroad. Her recent publications include the monograph *Gottfried Semper and the Problem of Historicism* (2004) and the anthology *Tracing Modernity* (2004). She is a contributing editor of the British journal *Architectural Research Quarterly* (ARQ).

THE DREAM OF PURE FORM

ICELANDIC RECEPTION OF MODERNIST THOUGHT AND ARCHITECTURE

Pétur Ármannsson

In Iceland, the introduction of concrete construction around 1900 had a special significance. For the first time, it became possible to build economical fireproof buildings out of local materials. Early on, concrete was used for private houses and public buildings, as well as factories and engineering constructions such as bridges. Conditions in Iceland were conducive to the modern movement and its new formal concept based on the properties of reinforced concrete, which by the year 1930 had become the most common method of building.[1]

With the Stockholm exhibition of 1930, the modern movement became the dominant force in Scandinavian architecture. The first houses in Iceland that clearly expressed modern esthetics were private residences in Reykjavik in the early 1930s. They were built of reinforced concrete with steel frame windows, corner openings, sun-terraces on flat, concrete roofs, and well balanced asymmetrical volumes. The most progressive developments of the new architecture can be found in private villas of well-to-do families in Reykjavik and housing groups financed and built by co-operative building unions.[2]

In the late 1930s, modern architecture was "vernacularized": it became the accepted norm in a simplified version.[3] During the Second World War, Iceland was disconnected from Scandinavia and mainland Europe. British and American troops were stationed in Iceland from 1940 onwards. Their activities brought prosperity to the local economy, as well as a strong cultural influence. The building boom during and after the war was a period of stagnation for modern architecture; the local, modern vernacular of the 1930s gradually lost its connection with progressive developments, the simple cubic forms of the 1930s disappeared, and houses were decorated with small window panes and ornamental railings.[4]

1 Pétur H. Ármannsson: "The development of Reykjavík in the 1920s and 1930s and the impact of functionalism," in: Wenche Findal (ed.): *Nordisk funksjonalisme: Det internasjonale og det nasjonale,* Oslo: Ad Notam Gyldendal, 1995, p. 47.

2 Júlíana Gottskálksdóttir: "Mellan tradition och förnuelse: Sigurdur Gudmundssons villor paa 1920- og 30-talet," in: Findal: *Nordisk funksjonalisme,* pp. 67-74.

3 Pétur H. Ármannsson: *Sigurður Guðmundsson arkitekt,* Reykjavík: Listasafn Reykjavíkur, 1997.

4 Pétur H. Ármannsson: "Social Aspects and Modern Architecture in Iceland," in: Ola Wedebrunn (ed.): *Modern Movement Scandinavia: Vision and Reality,* Aarhus: DOCOMOMO Nord, 1998, pp. 97-131.

The next step in the development of modern architecture occurs in the works of several young architects who came to work in Iceland in the period 1945-55, the majority of which were trained at the Royal Academy in Copenhagen. The first signs of what may be termed the "Pure Forms of 1950s Modernism" appeared in the midst of the Second World War. In 1940, two students of architecture, Gisli Halldorsson and Sigvaldi Thordarson, left Copenhagen with their families soon after the German occupation and managed to get on the very last ship leaving Scandinavia for Iceland in the fall of 1940. Back in Iceland, they established an architectural office which operated until 1947, at which point they went back to Copenhagen to finish their studies.[5]

In 1942, each of them designed their own house in a new suburb of Reykjavik, where we find a novel formal emphasis in the making. These one story, concrete block houses with a shed roof were in most respects different from the more traditional surrounding houses.[6] Thordarson divided the outer walls of his house into planes which were painted with contrasting primary colors, yellow and blue. Outer concrete walls had a smooth surface with sharp edges, painted in different colors. The side walls are different from the south side facing the garden, indicating a concrete frame with an infill of lighter elements, windows, and non-load bearing walls.[7]

The year 1945 saw the return of a number of Icelandic architects who had been stranded abroad during the war. One of them was Hannes Kr. Davidsson, who completed his studies in Copenhagen during the war. During the years 1946-47 he designed two residential buildings in Reykjavik, which in most respects were different from the local architecture at the time. They exhibit many characteristics that were to characterize Icelandic architecture during the 1950s and 1960s.[8]

5 Margrét Leifsdóttir: "Gísli Halldórsson og saga teiknistofunnar," in: Margrét Leifsdóttir (ed.): *Gísli Halldórsson arkitekt,* Reykjavík, 2009, p. 11-15.

6 Pétur H. Ármannsson: *Borgarhluti verður til: Byggingarlist og skipulag í Reykjavík eftirstríðsáranna* [Exhibition Catalogue], Reykjavík: Listasafn Reykjavíkur, 1999, pp. 4-5, 15.

7 Pétur H. Ármannsson: "Hreinstefna í húsagerð 6. áratugarins" = "Purism in 1950s Architecture," in: Ólafur Kvaran (ed.): *Draumurinn um hreint form. Íslensk abstraktlist 1950-60 = Dream of Pure Form: Icelandic Abstract Art 1950-1960,* Reykjavík: Listasafn Íslands, 1998, pp. 40-53.

8 Ibid., pp. 44-46.

A way of thinking about architecture differently to the 1930s is evident here, from cubic volumes with a continuous surface to a composition of two-dimensional planes and surfaces. The walls of these houses were painted, each side of the house is treated differently: load bearing side walls and between them a more open façade, often with an infill-frame of lighter materials, wood and glass. Like many Icelandic architects during and after the war, Davidsson was a student of Professor Edward Thomsen at the Academy in Copenhagen.[9]

The Danish architect Mogens Lassen was a pioneer in the design of apartment buildings of reinforced concrete. In 1937, Lassen, together with engineer Ernst Ishoy, designed and built the so-called System House in Copenhagen, with load bearing side walls and concrete floors in between. The enclosing exterior wall was non-load-bearing, made of light material: glass, panels and a light-weight frame. This framework gave the architect freedom, both in exterior design and spatial connection between inside and outside.[10] The transparent concept of construction with clear differentiation between load bearing walls and enclosing wall, was an important example for Davidsson and other young architects of the post-war generation in Iceland.[11]

Davidson's professor, Edward Thomsen, like Mogens Lassen, was among the first to use reinforced concrete in housing design in Denmark. Here, the structural frame was expressed in the architectural form, load bearing walls differed from infill walls, in contrast to the Icelandic way of using concrete. In this same issue of the magazine *Arkitekten*, there was example of an apartment building by Thomsen with the same structural principle as Mogens Lassen's System House, except that the side walls are placed at an angle to the street, giving the elevation a staggered profile which provides each balcony unit with more privacy and exposure to sunlight.[12]

9 Pétur H. Ármannsson: "Lífsverk í þágu byggingarlistar: arkitektinn Hannes Kr. Davídsson" [Lecture given at Reykjavik Art Museum, Kjarvalsstadir, 1 October 2004, not published].

10 Lisbet Balslev Jørgensen: *Arkitekten Mogens Lassen*, Copenhagen: Arkitektens Forlag, 1989, pp. 120–123.

11 Pétur H. Ármannsson: "Lífsverk í þágu byggingarlistar."

12 *Arkitekten maanedshæfte: Tidsskrift for Arkitektur og dekorativ kunst*, Copenhagen: Akademisk Arkitektforening, vol. 61, no. 10, 1939.

Instead of stressing the unity of adjoining wall planes with punctuated window openings, as was the custom in pre-war modern architecture, the house became a two-dimensional composition, reminiscent of abstract paintings. Such a composition might consist of smoothly sanded wall areas, painted in bright colors, clear-cut window openings containing large expanses of glass, and planes of different materials and textures, wood paneling, or natural rocks.

In 1947, Halldorsson and Thordarson completed their studies in Copenhagen. Sigvaldi Thordarson became very influential in Icelandic architecture of the 1950s. He produced work with strong formal characteristics, volumes of articulated planes in contrasting colors, as can be seen in drawings for a studio/villa in Reykjavik from 1949.[13] Halldorsson's own house, with the main apartment elevated on columns, was presented in a book on Nordic architecture published in connection with Nordisk Byggedag in Helsinki in 1955, as an example of new, progressive architecture.[14]

Thordarson was very active from the early 1950s until his premature death in 1964. He became known for his innovative housing solutions. An important example of this is the apartment block in Reykjavik, designed for the Building Union of Government officials. It departs from the box-like form of other post war apartment buildings, broken into connected units, which are placed on a diagonal, allowing daylight from four directions in all apartments.[15] An equally innovative solution for terrace housing, which became increasingly popular in the 1950s, was the terrace house as a sculptural object placed diagonally to the street line, creating a strong sense of rhythm, most likely inspired by Arne Jacobsen's terrace housing at Söholm, Klampenborg, 1950-55.[16]

The tendency in Icelandic architecture of the 1950's towards clearly defined planes and surfaces, formal clarity, and the use of color to bring life to space and volume cannot be associated with the personal approach of any one architect in particular. Several Icelandic architects at the time were thinking along similar lines; One could

13 Water-color drawing of Kvisthagi 13, Reykjavík. Sigvaldi Thordarson's collection, National Archives of Iceland.

14 *Nordisk Arkitektur 1950-1954,* Helsinki: Nordisk Bygnadsdag VI, 1955.

15 Hörður Bjarnason: *Íslenzk íbúðarhús,* Reykjavík: Almenna bókafélagid, 1959, p. 118-119.

16 Terrace housing, Ljósheimar 1-7, Reykjavík. Sigvaldi Thordarson's collection, National Archives of Iceland.

talk about a school of thought or a trend.[17] Until the 1950s, most Icelandic architects had been trained in Denmark. In the postwar period, architects started to seek education in other countries. In 1953, Guðmundur Kr. Kristinsson finished his professional training at ETH in Zürich and came to practice in Iceland. He was to become one of the leading modern architects of the 1950s and 1960s. Kristinsson's early work shared some of the formal characteristics that were becoming common in Icelandic architecture, with composed planes and openings in what was essentially a solid, concrete construction.[18]

During the 1950s, there was a clear correlation between the formal concerns of Icelandic architecture on the one hand and those of contemporary Icelandic artists on the other. There are obvious connections between the geometric abstraction practiced by several young painters and the architects striving towards what we could call "Pure Form."[19] A key person in this regard was the painter and architecture critic Hörður Ágústsson, who studied visual art in Copenhagen and Paris just after the war.

Ágústsson was one of the founding members of the Icelandic Art Review "Birtingur" in 1955. He was very critical of the lack of sophistication in mainstream postwar architecture in Iceland, which he linked with the cultural degradation caused by the 1940 military occupation of Iceland with all its implications, particularly the breaking of long-standing cultural ties with Danish visual art from which Iceland had long benefited.[20] Ágústsson was very much in favor of the new tendency of younger architects towards "Pure Form," he believed that this new visual language of art, architecture, and design should really be a natural part of everyday life. True to that belief, he worked simultaneously as a visual artist, graphic designer – making books, posters and advertisements – and interior decorator.[21]

17 Pétur H. Ármannsson: "Hreinstefna í húsagerð 6. áratugarins" = "Purism in 1950s Architecture," p. 47.

18 Ibid., p. 40.

19 Ibid., p. 41.

20 Hörður Ágústsson: "Byggingarlist VIII," in: *Birtingur,* Reykjavík, no. 3, 1960, p. 28.

21 Pétur H. Ármannsson: "Opening the eyes of a Nation: Hördur Ágústsson´s contribution to architecture," in: Pétur H. Ármannsson (ed.): *Hördur Ágústsson – Endurreisnarmaður íslenskra sjónmennta* [Exhibition Catalogue], Reykjavík: Listasafn Reykjavíkur, 2005, p. 32-37.

A notable further practitioner of pure form was architect Skarphedinn Johannsson, not least because of his personal connections with leading Scandinavian architects and designers. He was originally trained as a furniture designer in Denmark in the 1930s, at the same time as Hans J. Wegner, a good friend of his. After the war, Johannsson went to study architecture in Copenhagen. During and after his studies, he worked for Professor Kaare Klint, but in 1952 he moved to Reykjavik and established his own office.[22] Johannsson was Alvar Aalto's representative in Iceland during the construction of the Nordic House in the 1960s.

It is appropriate to conclude with the building of the Nordic House in Reykjavik by the Finnish architect Alvar Aalto. Commissioned in 1963 and completed in 1968, this building is without doubt one of the most significant events in Iceland in the twentieth century. Aalto was the only "Great Master" of modern architecture to visit Iceland and work on commissions there. The governments of the five Nordic countries were jointly responsible for erecting the building. A decision was made not to conduct a competition but to award the project directly to the world-renowned Finnish architect. The program was for a small cultural center with a library of Nordic books, a lecture room, cafeteria, and offices for university lecturers in Scandinavian languages. The Nordic House was a cultural-political statement, intended to reconnect Iceland with Scandinavian culture, old and new, and in so doing counteract the strong influence of Anglo-Saxon popular culture, which had prevailed in Iceland during and after the war. To make such a statement in the form of a great work of architecture became the key to its success.[23]

About the author
Pétur H. Ármannsson is Curator of Architecture at Reykjavik Art Museum and visiting professor and lecturer at Iceland Academy of the Arts. He studied architecture at the University of Toronto, Canada and undertook postgraduate work at Cornell University, Ithaca, New York, obtaining his M.A. in 1990. He worked as an architect in the studio of Dagny Helgadottir and Gudni Palsson, Reykjavik and as the director of the Architecture Department, Reykjavik Art Museum from 1993 to 2006. Armannsson is the author of numerous texts and media programs on twentieth century architecture in Iceland.

22 Haraldur Helgason (ed): *Arkitektatal.* Reykjavík: Þjóðsaga, 1997, pp. 452-453.

23 Pétur H. Ármannsson: "Aallon näkemys Reykjavíkista" = "Aalto's Vision of Reykjavík" in: Haraldur Helgason, Málfríður Kristjánsdóttir and Pétur H. Ármannsson (eds.): *Nordic House: Alvar Aalto: Iceland = Pohojan Talo: Alvar Aalto: Islanti.* Reykjavík: Norræna húsid, 1999, pp. 55-68.

GOING SOUTH

DANISH AND NORDIC "EMPIRICISM" AND ITS REPRESENTATION AT INTERBAU IN 1957

Nils-Ole Lund

In 1950, Bruno Zevi, the Italian writer on architecture, published his book *Towards an Organic Architecture.* His theme was not the conflict between tradition and modernity, but rather the conflict between two ways of being modern: one could advocate either Mies van der Rohe's modernist classicism or Frank Lloyd Wright's organic way of thinking. As the title of the book indicated, Zevi was an adherent of the latter view of architecture, and he saw that,

> [...] in the USA, the organic architecture of Sullivan and Wright has benefited from contact with the ideas of European architects. A new architectural movement has grown through this joint influence. Its most important characteristics, though obtained through different processes and for different reasons, can be found widely from Scandinavia to Japan, and are clearly apparent in the outlook on life of many young architects.[1]

The situation in Scandinavia was therefore, in Zevi's view, a promising one. He was thinking first and foremost of the buildings Aalto and Markelius had designed for the World Fairs of the 1930s. Functionalism, as modernism or the new objectivity was called in Scandinavia, had a more human scale than Central European architecture.

During World War Two, Finland and Norway had suffered great devastation in their northern areas. Denmark and Sweden, on the other hand, had managed to escape without major damage. In all these countries, building had been affected by lack of materials. But the language of form had also reacted against the harsh realities, by cultivating traditional features such as double-pitched roofs and using materials such as unplastered bricks and wood. In 1950, Kay Fisker, the architect who dominated the Danish architectural scene at the time, wrote in an article on the situation:

> We discuss monumentality, the sterility of functionalism, the new empiricism, the Bay Region style and Marxist architecture without, it seems, achieving anything but further confusion. We tire of clichés such as "organic", "spontaneous" and "humane" architecture; we wonder at the mysticism of Aulis

1 Bruno Zevi: *Towards an Organic Architecture,* London: Faber and Faber, 1950, p.11.

> Blomstedt and Reinius. All over the world we see attempts to attenuate the cold functionalism of the 1930s by adding a touch of picturesque detail, as in the case of the Swedes, or a little ornamentation, as in the case of the Dutch. There is a lot of imagining, poetic invention and dreaming, often leading to the most bizarre results.[2]

In opposition to this architectural confusion, Fisker put forward his own position, which he called "the functional tradition"; besides international functionalism there was a domestic tradition, in which closed forms and the texture of materials were cultivated. Fisker took the term from the British periodical *The Architectural Review,* where it had been used in a somewhat different sense.

In the course of the 1950s, however, the situation improved. Young Scandinavian architects once again began to travel abroad to study what had been happening during their time of isolation. They went first and foremost to the USA, where the architecture of the west coast was of particular interest to them. In this way, European modernism came back to its original home, but in an American version devoid of the social message of functionalism.

The architects also traveled to the Mediterranean countries and Mexico to learn from the anonymous buildings "without architects" and the pre-Colombian ruins. They were not only looking for the modern; they were also attracted by the primitive. The experiences of the architects merged with the Nordic tradition of good craftsmanship, and the concept of Scandinavian Design was created. The end of the 1950s has since been called a Golden Age, at least in Denmark. At the same time, Sweden was one of the richest countries in Europe, and a model of how the state could influence the development of society. The growth of Stockholm was to be regulated by concentrating urban development in satellite townships divided into neighborhood units in the British manner and connected with the center by underground railways.

The architecture that was to leave its mark on the new Swedish towns was, however, less consistent and, unlike the town planning, was not internationally admired. In those years Norway did not play any major international role, and Norway did not

2 *Arkitektens månedshæfte,* no. 5-6, 1950, p. 100.

participate in the Interbau. In Finland, Alvar Aalto was the dominant figure, and internationally always acted as the representative of Finnish architecture and culture. In 1950-52 he built a small town hall in Säynätsalo in central Finland, a building which, in time, came to stand for the best in Nordic architecture, excelling in features such as adaptation to the site, textural features of materials used (copper, wood, and tiles), modest scale, and democratic layout of a public institution.

What happened in the best part of Scandinavian architecture in these years, before industrialization took over with its mass building, was that a bridge was built over the gap, which, in Kay Fisker's words, existed between tradition and internationalism. Inspiration from outside gave life to the art of building in the Scandinavian countries, with names such as Utzon, Lewerentz, Jacobsen, and Aalto.

As we have seen, in the postwar years the Scandinavian architects learned principally from the USA, where the Bauhaus architects had been exiled. With respect to town planning, it was England that was their model. Germany was, for obvious reasons, not a suitable place for study.

Until 1933, Germany, and especially Berlin, had been the place where new trends were available for inspection. Kay Fisker therefore visited Berlin, in 1928 and 1931.[3] In 1928 it was Mendelsohn's horizontal window bands that made such a deep impression on him that, on his return, he immediately changed the façades of a block of flats that he was building by the lakes in Copenhagen. In 1931, the big construction exhibition was the main object of his visit, but on his way home he met a group of architects at the school in Bernau by Hannes Meyer, a design that became a model for Danish architects up to the 1950s, because of its adaption to the sloping terrain and its matter-of-fact functionality. If one studies Fisker's diaries, one can see what was most important for him in Berlin: meeting Bruno Taut, Erich Mendelsohn, and Heinrich Tessenow. Here, the 1950 issue of tradition or international modernism was already evident. All his life, Fisker had a foot in both camps, but his sympathy probably lay first and foremost with Tessenow's modest houses, which were so close to the provincial architecture that Fisker had surveyed in his youth.

3 These visits to Berlin are described by Nils-Ole Lund in *Bygmesteren C.F. Møller*, Aarhus: Aarhus universitetsforlag, 1998, pp. 42-43.

Another Danish architect who was well connected with Germany and who also admired Tessenow was Steen Eiler Rasmussen. As late as 1973, when he was awarded the Tessenow Medal, he said "Tessenow's modest architecture of yesterday can show the way to a healthy architecture for tomorrow."[4] Rasmussen had in 1940 published the book *Nordische Baukunst,* which, however, dealt only with Sweden and Denmark. The book made no mention of Denmark's best-known architect, the modernist Arne Jacobsen, and the title of the last chapter was "Bescheidenheit eine Zier" (Modesty a Virtue), a somewhat peculiar sentiment to express in German, in 1940, after the occupation of Denmark. But it may be explained by, among other things, Rasmussen's admiration for Tessenow's architecture.

Tessenow did not become a Nazi, but he was greatly admired by Albert Speer. However, there was a great distance between the gigantic neo-classicism of Hitler and Speer, and Tessenow's unostentatious and subdued Hellerup houses. As a student, Speer had been in Copenhagen, and he appreciated the Danish neo-classicism of the 1920s, but when, in 1941, he presented his own projects in the very same city, the reaction was mixed for both political and architectural reasons. Denmark was occupied, and nobody knew which side would win. People were intimidated by the large-scale projects, and criticism was muted.

The town planning and architectural views of the Nazis were also marked, however, by a predilection for everything rustic and medieval.[5] Himmler and Rosenberg were the leading advocates of this anti-classical attitude. So strangely, both in Danish architecture and in the German architecture of the 1930s, there was a split between the cultivation of tradition and the importation of an idealized, foreign architecture, whether it was neo-classicism or functionalism. This schism between tradition and modernism is perhaps concealed by modernism being dressed in a universal historical costume. Indeed, in Nazism the split took rather perverted forms.

In 1930, when Swedish architects, without any reservations, switched to functionalism, their Danish colleagues were more sceptical. Both Kay Fisker and Steen Eiler

4 Olaf Lind: *Arkitekten Steen Eiler Rasmussen,* Copenhagen: Gyldendal, 2008, p. 78. In the chapter "Tyske venner," pp. 74-84, Lind describes Rasmussen's German connections.

5 See Barbara Miller Lane: *National Romanticism and Modern Architecture in Germany and the Scandinavian Countries,* Cambridge: Cambridge University Press, 2000, pp. 303-311.

Rasmussen were unconvinced by the way that modernism and functionalism insisted on the dominance of function. Both were critical towards Bauhaus, and Rasmussen thought that le Corbusier was primarily an esthete. Nor was Arne Jacobsen, Denmark's leading modernist, included in *Nordische Baukunst* in 1940.

In the postwar years, when the German architects began the reconstruction of their bombed cities, they looked abroad for inspiration.[6] In Sweden they found an approach to town-planning based on welfare virtues such as social awareness and democratic decision-making. In Denmark they saw an architecture that was both unostentatious and modern. In 1954, therefore, both Kay Fisker and Arne Jacobsen were invited to participate in the planned Interbau exhibition in the Tiergarten district of Berlin.

The construction plan, which determined where they were to build, was influenced by the purpose of showing what international architecture in the West could do. A number of architects participated with projects which were incompatible with one another. These projects were essentially "exhibition stands" where interpretations of postwar modernism were to be presented. In one Danish account, the construction was characterized as a "collection of brilliant, but at times also ecstatic, architectural demonstrations." As for Kay Fisker's building, "short-term exhibition considerations had not been allowed to distort its features."[7] It was a further development of a type of home that had been designed for a Copenhagen suburb a few years earlier, a combination of terraced houses and balcony access blocks. Below there were terraced houses, and above them flats with access from a balcony. The materials used for the partition walls and façades were reused bricks from the ruins of Berlin.

According to the architect, it was a building where the rent was the lowest in all the Hansaviertel, but it was not an epoch-making piece of architecture.[8] And in the 1968 guide-book to essential buildings in Berlin, there is no reproduction of Kay Fisker's house, whereas Arne Jacobsen's contribution to Interbau is represented. This was also of modest extent: four single-family houses, three of them with court-

6 The discussion of Berlin's town planning is reported in Hans Helge Madsen: *Saglighedens Slagmark,* Copenhagen: Munksgaard/ Rosinante, 1997.

7 Both quotations are from Hans Erling Langkilde: *Arkitekten Kay Fisker,* Copenhagen: Arkitekten, 1960, p. 92.

8 The design is published in *Arkitekten,* no. 15, 1958, pp. 244-247.

yards. In the case of Jacobsen, too, it was an adaptation of a type of home built in Denmark. In those years, the courtyard-house was developed into a modern version of a very old type of home, which combined a modest plot size with access to a private garden.

The houses were built of concrete elements and wooden patios produced in Denmark. In form as well as in construction, Arne Jacobsen's houses were more modern than Kay Fisker's.[9] And in fact Jacobsen was given several commissions in Germany in the following years.

About the author

Nils-Ole Lund, professor emeritus, graduated from the Royal Academy's School of Architecture in Copenhagen in 1953. He worked as an architect and professor in both Sweden and Norway, and was a professor at the Aarhus School of Architecture, where he was rector from 1972 to 1985. He was president of the Society of European Architectural Schools until 1991. His specialty is the history of modern architecture, and he has written many books on the subject: *Teoridannelser i arkitekturen* (1970) and *Artitekturteorier siden 1945* (2001), as well as *Nordic Architecture* (2008) have become standard works of architecture history.

9 The design is published in *Arkitekten,* no. 5, 1959, pp. 85-87.

"TEAR IT DOWN!"

EXAMINATION OF THE DISCOURSES IN SUBURB CRITIQUE

Lisbeth Söderqvist

Welfare for All in the New Towns

This is a tale of the postwar constructed environments that arose as the European welfare states took shape.[1] When these environments were planned and built, they offered an attractive alternative to the traditional town, associated with the more undesirable aspects of capitalism and urban growth.

The "new towns" were initially regarded as an expression of the modern welfare state, but during the 1960s they came to be used as targets for general social criticism. In discussions in Sweden today, they are often used by architects as an illustration of the disastrous consequences of allowing the wrong planning principles to prevail. They claim that the new towns are badly designed, and that this is one of the main reasons why they are characterized by ethnic segregation and poverty.

In this article, I want to propagate a different tale of the new towns. My starting point is not that they are badly designed, and/or an expression of a misguided housing policy; instead, I want to describe the ideas and thoughts behind their development. I will also analyze the critics' arguments. The question is: what are they really saying?

As has been noted by other researchers, the segregation that is now at the center of the new town discussion both influences and is influenced by local perceptions; it clings to the people who live there. It is important to bear this in mind when we write and describe the new towns.[2]

Postwar Town Planning Ideals: Small Towns Divided Into Neighborhood Units

After the Second World War, many town planners made use of the principle known as neighborhood planning, which became the twentieth century's predominant planning principle and had its roots in sociology, rather a fashionable discipline in the postwar era. Sociologists considered that the primary group, consisting of family, friends,

---

1 This article is based on the book by Lisbeth Söderqvist: *Att gestalta välfärd. Från idé till byggd miljö.* Stockholm: Forskningsrådet Formas och Riksantikvarieämbetet, 2008.

2 Kerstin Bodström: "Värdet på förortsbörsen," in: Gun Frank (ed.): *Spelet om staden,* Stockholm: Formas, 2005, pp. 145-158.

and neighbors was of great importance to the individual's social development. The inclusive interpersonal relations, which were developed face to face, in small groups, were assumed to form the basis of social cohesion.[3] In large towns, it was difficult for people to build social networks, according to the sociologists. People became isolated and rootless and, in extreme cases, even criminal and asocial. Here was a chance, it was thought, for planners and architects to contribute, firstly by building new towns with relatively few inhabitants, and secondly by dividing these towns into still smaller units, so-called neighborhood units, so that processes of socialization would be facilitated by the nature of the physical environment.

Traffic Segregation

In the decades after the Second World War, traffic routes and streets were planned to a large extent on the basis of what is known as the principle of traffic segregation. There was widespread support for the idea of abandoning the traditional type of road network. In the 1930s, the international organisation CIAM (Les Congrès Internationaux d'Architecture Moderne), which attracted many architects with an intrerest in architecture and planning, drew up a set of guidelines for "the functional city." This was disseminated primarily during the 1940s. Key ingredients included: parallel residential blocks with large unbuilt but planted areas in between, and separated from the road network; as well as multi-story blocks, terraced housing, recreation areas between the buildings (playgrounds, parks, sports grounds, etc.); and intersection-free traffic routes.[4]

3 Nils Mortensen: "Den amerikanska pragmatismen," in: Heine Andersen and Lars Bo Kaspersen (eds.): *Klassisk och modern samhällsteori,* Lund: Studentlitteratur, 2003, pp. 149-150.

4 This guideline was regarded as the most genuine expression of modernism. See José Luis Sert: *Can Our Cities Survive? An ABC of Urban Problems, Their Analyses, Their Solutions: Based on the Proposals Formulated by the CIAM,* Cambridge: Harvard University Press, 1942.

Industrialization and the Standardization of Construction

At the end of the Second World War, many European countries were faced with the task of extensive reconstruction; not least, new housing was needed. State subsidies and preferential loans were given to the construction industry to enable it to develop new building methods. Up until the 1940s and 1950s, building was still done manually, and appeared almost antiquated in contrast with other spheres of labor. By modernizing the methods used, it would be possible to increase the speed of production. The aim was to provide cheap, good-quality homes relatively quickly.[5] The mode of production did not automatically determine the look of the buildings; although this was in some cases an uncompromising expression of the production process, architects chose in other cases to tone down this aspect. In other words, architectural values, rather than technology per se, were decisive in determining the result.[6]

Great Britain and the New Towns Program

The principle of building new towns divided into neighborhood units was applied in many countries. New towns were built in Germany, France, Italy, Hungary, the Soviet Union, Scandinavia, the USA, and Israel. The best-known is Brasilia in South America. But for the majority of people, Great Britain is probably most closely associated with this development. The plans for London in particular (1943 and 1945) were circulated and read with great interest by planners in other countries. Many of them also traveled to Britain to conduct field studies.

According to the Labour government, which took the decision to build the new towns in 1946, they were to be socially balanced, meaning that in each town there should be different types of housing and workplaces for people with different levels of income and education. One important ingredient was that the neighborhoods should

5 Selective housing allowances for families and general subsidies for housing production were proposed by the Social Housing Commission, SOU, 1945: 63.

6 Brian Finnimore: *Houses From the Factory: System Building and the Welfare State 1942-74*, London: Rivers Oram Press, 1989.

have places for their inhabitants to meet. The interaction which arose in the district's central meeting place, called the "community center," was an important component; this was where the sense of community, which sociologists considered to be of such importance for the individual, would be generated. Without this there was a risk that people would end up on the margins of society, or else form sub-groups with hostile attitudes to one another, such as class hatred.[7] Society could counteract these tendencies by planning towns for socio-economic integration, with places for people to meet and interact.

British Stevenage and Swedish Vällingby

Stevenage New Town was one of the very first new towns to be built in Great Britain from the end of the 1940s onwards. It was planned for 60,000 inhabitants: six neighborhoods with 10,000 inhabitants each.[8] The project gained a reputation and attracted many visitors, including some from Sweden.[9] It is well known that the architects who took part in the planning of Vällingby in Stockholm were in close contact with the British planners involved in the development of Stevenage.[10] Vällingby is a contemporary equivalent of Stevenage. Like the British example, the new town of Vällingby was divided into a number of neighborhood units.[11] The town center, Vällingby *centrum*, was given a location approximately in the middle of the new town.

7 These aspects of societal development are discussed by such American sociologists as Lloyd Warner and the so-called Chicago School of sociologists. Maurice B. Stein: *Identity and Anxiety: Survival of the Person in Mass Society,* New York: Free Press, 1960, pp. 8-9, pp. 91-92.

8 *Building the New Town of Stevenage.* Hertfordshire: Stevenage Development Corporation, Hertfordshire, 1954, p. 9.

9 Peter Self: "Introduction: new towns in the modern world," in: Hazel Evans (ed.): *New Towns: The British Experience,* London: C. Knight for the Town and Planning Association, 1972, pp. 1-10.

10 Ulrika Sax: *Vällingby, ett levande drama,* Stockholm: Stockholmia, 1998, p. 90, and a lecture by Ulrika Sax at a conference at Stockholms Stadsmuseum, 6 December 2004.

11 Grimsta is often not mentioned. The fact that Grimsta was one of the well-known neighborhoods in Vällingby is mentioned by David Pass, *Vällingby and Farsta: From Ideas to Reality,* Cambridge, Mass.: MIT Press, 1973, p. 13.

It was planned that the total population would reach 60,000,[12] the same as in Stevenage.

Both Stevenage and Vällingby included workplaces as well as dwellings for various groups with different levels of education and income, which was regarded by the Britons as a necessary precondition for social integration and social stability.[13] This idea was by no means self-evident; in the 1940s, there were those who expressed an ambivalent view of the idea of mixing different socioeconomic groups. But postwar residential areas in Sweden generally follow the Vällingby model, with housing for various social classes. There were meeting places, corresponding to the British community centers, both in the new town's large central complex, the "town center", and in the smaller center complexes in each neighborhood unit.[14]

There was a discussion in Great Britain concerning how far from the nearest large town the new towns could be built. There were those who favored relatively large and completely independent towns at a considerable distance from the old town centers, a viewpoint familiar to Swedish architects from the widely-circulated publication *Nutida engelsk samhällsplanering* (Contemporary Community Planning in England).[15] One problem, though, was that the further away the new towns were, the less easy, presumably, it would be to attract people to move there from the old ones. There was no question of forcing them to move, either in Great Britain or in Sweden. For this reason, many of the new towns were eventually located relatively close to the older urban centers. Cumbernauld New Town, for example, is situated some sixteen to twenty kilometers from the center of Glasgow. The journey by local train takes twenty-five minutes, almost exactly the same journey time as between Stockholm central station

12 "Hemmen och samhällsplaneringen," SOU [Statens offentliga utredningar; Swedish Government Official Reports] 1956: 32, p. 137 (quotation from *Byggmästaren* 1956, no. 3). This is how architect Sven Markelius describes Vällingby. The Swedish planners generally used the term "district" (stadsdel) for what I am here calling "neighborhood unit" (grannskapsenhet).

13 The head office of the power company Statliga Vattenfall was located in the new town, as was that of Svenska Bostäder (the future proprietor of Vällingby center). The carriage depot of SL, the public transport provider for Stockholm county, was also built here. In Johannelund, next to Vällingby, there is an industrial and office zone. In addition, there were all the job opportunities offered by the shops in the town center. Sax: *Vällingby, ett levande drama*, p. 12.

14 Sax: *Vällingby, ett levande drama*, pp. 110-113, pp. 125-128.

15 Otto Danneskiold-Samsøe: *Nutida engelsk samhällsplanering*, Stockholm: Forum, 1945.

and Vällingby. In the case of Stockholm, another factor was that the planners had to stick within local government boundaries. Vällingby borders on the municipality of Järfälla, and was therefore as far out as the Stockholm Town-Building Office could operate at that time.[16]

The 1960s: The New Town of Skärholmen

In Stockholm, Vällingby was followed by the new towns of Farsta and Skärholmen, which followed more or less the same pattern. It is perhaps surprising that Vällingby is commonly described as a success, while Skärholmen was immediately declared a failure.

Skärholmen is situated on the southwestern outskirts of Stockholm, bordering on the municipality of Huddinge. The planning of the area began in the mid 1950s, just after the official opening of Vällingby in 1954.[17] It was estimated that the population would reach about 55,000,[18] roughly the same as many of the British new towns planned in the 1940s or Vällingby. Like Vällingby, Skärholmen offered various types of housing; single family houses accounted for a third of the dwellings.[19] The plans

16 Half of the parish of Spånga was incorporated into Stockholm in 1949, allowing for expansion of Vällingby. Marianne Råberg: "Stockholms Ytterstad," in: Göran Söderström and Elisabeth Jermsten (eds.): *Stockholm utanför tullarna. Nittiosju stadsdelar i ytterstaden*, Stockholm: Stockholmia, 2004, pp. 11-32, p. 27.

17 Memorandum of 8 November 1956 concerning plans for investigation of the possibility of developing Sätra-Vårby and Brännkyrka-Huddinge. Document in housing authority archives, Stockholm Town-Building Office, Pl 5009. See also Stockholm Regional Planning Board: *Förslag till Regionplan för Stockholmstrakten 1958*, Stockholm: Seelig, 1958, map supplement B, which shows that the structural plan for the area was ready at that date. It may be noted, however, that the large central complex on the map is situated in what was to become Sätra, and not Skärholmen.

18 "Beskrivning till principförslag till generalplan för del av Skärholmen-Vårby," dated 28.06.1962, in housing authority archives, Stockholm Town-Building Office, Pl 5010, "Beskrivning till generalplan för stadsdelarna Skärholmen och Vårberg i Stockholm," dated 12.09.1963, in housing authority archives, Stockholm Town-Building Office, Pl 5010.

19 According to the documentation accompanying the plans, it was intended that 30 percent of the population of Skärholmen would live in terraced or detached houses. Stockholm Central Board of Administration's report and memorandum, no. 44, 1961. Copy in housing authority archives, Stockholm Town-Building Office, Pl 5009, "Beskrivning till generalplan för stadsdelarna Skärholmen och Vårberg i Stockholm," Pl 5010.

also included separate old people's homes, nursing homes, and housing for pensioners. There were plenty of workplaces in this part of Stockholm, and new ones were added; the plans for the new town included land earmarked for offices and light industry, and employment opportunities arose as the town grew; the shops in the center had to be staffed, as did old people's homes, schools, and other public services.

It is a reasonable interpretation to say that the ideal of integrating different socio-economic groups as well as young and old people is reflected in the plan, and that the aim was to create a socially balanced community with housing and employment for various social classes and groups, roughly along the lines formulated by British politicians and planners in the 1940s. This goal had also, as we have seen, played a key role in the designing of Vällingby. Other similarities can be mentioned: both projects applied the principles of neighborhood planning and traffic segregation. The latter means, as we have seen, that traffic is not routed into residential areas, but rather diverted round them.

There were many similarities between Vällingby and Skärholmen, but they differed in two respects. The Stockholm Chamber of Commerce recommended that Skärholmen should have 4,000-5,000 parking spaces, and this number was in fact provided.[20] At about the same time, Vällingby had only 1,000. Furthermore, the area occupied by shops in the center of Skärholmen was considerably larger than in Vällingby. In 1968, when Skärholmen was opened, there were some 53,000 square meters of retail floor space. By comparison, plans for Vällingby in the late 1940s had provided for a central complex with only 3,300 square meters of floor space. The difference, according to a survey made before the planning of Skärholmen, was due to people's increased purchasing power. New goods and demands had arisen, and mass production meant that goods that had once been beyond the reach of all but a small proportion of consumers were now, in the 1960s, affordable for almost anyone. The rapid rise in car ownership had also influenced shopping habits; distance to shops had become less significant to customers, and this was to the advantage of large central retail complexes.

20 Letter to Josef Stäck, 29.01.1963, in housing authority archives, Stockholm Town-Building Office, Pl 5010.

People were attracted to these by the greater range of goods they offered. The same development was also seen in other countries.[21]

The plans for Skärholmen included numerous places of assembly: restaurants, cafes, meeting rooms, a Free Church (as well as the state church), a theater/cinema, premises for the Workers' Educational Association, a bowling hall, a swimming pool and sports hall, among others. No one in the new town was to be deprived of social services such as health and dental care, a labor exchange, police station, and post office.[22] There were extensive unbuilt areas for outdoor activities, and a so-called outdoor center. Sports fields, a harbor for pleasure boats, a campsite, and two open-air swimming pools were also included in the plan, as were eight play centers and large playgrounds with equipment and staff. There were also a riding school, footpaths for rambling, a cycle path, and a shooting range. Each neighborhood also had a church, library, schools, youth center, day nurseries, and kindergartens. In Bredäng, an indoor swimming pool was built at more or less the same time as the housing. In Skärholmen, plans for an indoor swimming pool came to fruition in the 1980s.

The Skärholmen Debate

When Skärholmen center was opened in 1968, a critical debate, commonly called the Skärholmen debate, broke out in the press.[23] The most frequently cited passage

21 The retail trade association of Stockholm city and county, which took part in the survey, referred to statistics gathered in Sweden and abroad, and to experiences from Vällingby center, but also from American and European conurbations. Statement by the retail trade association of Stockholm city and county, 12.06.1963, in housing authority archives, Stockholm Town-Building Office, Pl 5010.

22 Stockholm Town-Building Office, Pl 5010 "Situationsplan" 22.02.1963; undated working document by architects' firm of Willhelm Boijsen and Dag Efverdal with the heading "Fritid," in housing authority archives, Stockholm Town-Building Office, Pl 6235; Allan Westerman: "Utvecklingen efter Årsta," in: *Arkitektur,* 1965, pp. 267-276.

23 According to the library service agency's publication *Svenska Tidningsartiklar,* the Skärholmen debate consisted of twenty-seven articles published in the daily press during a three-month period at the end of 1968. But there were also other articles in which Skärholmen was discussed in various ways, even though not all of them can be said to have Skärholmen as their main topic. I made a preliminary selection of 55 articles from daily newspapers, of which 20 are referred to in the text. The majority, as will be clear from the selection hereunder, were published in three newspapers: *Dagens Nyheter, Expressen,* and *Svenska Dagbladet.*

from this debate is probably one published in the daily *Dagens Nyheter* two days after the opening, and written by the author and literary critic Lars-Olof Franzén: "Tear Skärholmen down. [...] The only thing you can use Skärholmen for is rolling bottles to make one hell of a noise between the walls. Tear it down!" The dramatist Margareta Garpe called Skärholmen "the concentration camp of the welfare state."[24]

The art critic Ulf Hård af Segerstad was among those who, in a series of articles in Svenska Dagbladet, sharply criticized the design of Skärholmen. In his view, Skärholmen did not offer "opportunities for individual self-realization." "This is not a society built for people of balanced psycho-physical development in a living social environment; it is a consumer center for the crippled version of humanity [...] that could be called four-wheel man."

Ulf Hård af Segerstad thought that Skärholmen forced people to live a life marked by consumption and car travel: consumption, because Skärholmen was "a society for compulsive buyers"; and car travel, because Skärholmen was to a large extent suited to the needs of motorists, which forced people to travel by car. These twin compulsions deformed people both mentally and physically: mentally, because the forces of commerce drove people into conformism and threatened individual development; and physically, because the design of the town forced people into driving. [25]

Marxism and the Critique of Consumption

In capitalist society, people were alienated and deprived of the chance to create an authentic life for themselves – this was one of the messages of the left-wing intellectuals who, as is well known, had largely taken the initiative in problem formulation at the time in question. Many adherents of western Marxism, which constituted an alternative to the form of Marxism developed in the east, emphasized exactly this vulnerability of the individual; this has been described as the "humanization" of Marx.

24 Ann Hellman: "Skärholmen – myt och verklighet," in: Ulrika Sax (ed.): *Miljonprogram i Stockholm*, Stockholm: Stockholms stadsmuseum, 2000, pp. 112-119, p. 113.

25 Source for this extract and the one immediately above: Ulf Hård af Segerstad: "Den fyrhjuliga människan – stadens sabotör," in: *Svenska Dagbladet*, 14.09.1968.

Marx was interpreted as a philosopher who focused his attention on the individual, rather than being a social theorist.[26] The "thousand Marxisms," cross-fertilized with structuralism and phenomenology, and with its roots in the interwar period, were disseminated during the 1950s, and during the following decade Marx was read and interpreted by growing numbers of people. There arose variants of Marxism such as Maoism and Trotskyism, to name but two well-known examples.[27]

If I assume that our relationship with reality is expressed through our conception of how the world is constructed, Ulf Hård af Segerstad's wording can be interpreted as being permeated with Marxist ideology. This does not mean that he must have been a Marxist, but rather that he was caught in a frame of thinking that was widespread at the time. An alternative interpretation is that his criticism is an expression of a culturally conservative stance. Both cultural conservatives and Marxists argue that consumption, as a phenomenon, is characterized by manipulation; the basis for this argument is an analysis intended to show that we do not actually need all the goods we buy, but are manipulated into consumption.[28]

As can be seen from the article referred to above, Ulf Hård af Segerstad regards the commercial element in the town-center complex, and motoring, as direct threats to the individual. The great range of goods on offer in the shops, and the car, are regarded as negative expressions of mass production and technical rationality. This caused the disintegration of the individual, which, according to Marx's interpreters, led to alienation. They thought that people in a technological society became alienated from their work, from themselves, from society and from nature.

26 Based on Sven-Erik Liedman: *En värld att vinna. Aspekter på den unge Karl Marx*, Stockholm: Bonnier, 1968, p. 120, pp. 205-206. In the notes on page 205 he names a number of authors who contributed to this "humanization".

27 Per Månsson: "Marxism," in: Andersen and Kaspersen (eds.): *Klassisk och modern samhällsteori*, 2003, pp. 42-52.

28 Peder Aléx: "Vägra konsumera? Nedslag i konsumtionens idéhistoria," lecture, University of Umeå, [209.85.129.132/search?q=cache:YJ4ViDkECZcJ:www8.umu.se/humfak/kansliet/alex_peder_docforel.html+Vägra+konsumera&cd=3&hl=sv&ct=clnk&gl=se], December 2005 [cache-version 6.04.2009]

Shops and cars were projected into symbols of a society where the individual could not live an authentic life, but became, as Segerstad expresses it, deformed, by – it is implied – consumer society.

To Live or To Buy?

Olle Bengtzon was a journalist on the daily newspaper *Expressen* who wrote almost exclusively about housing issues. For him, the architecture of Skärholmen center was a problem. The scale of it was "inhuman," with "enormous shop-windows" and "huge roofs." Only a few people – completely at the mercy of the powers of commerce – were to be seen in the desolate "temple-court of Mammon," as Bengtzon calls Skärholmen. He uses this expression to say that the planners and builders of Skärholmen were in the hands of capitalism, or "Mammon." He describes the architecture as exaggeratedly variegated, sumptuous and commercial: "every bit as gaudy and extravagant as the goods sold there." He pleads for a more intimate architecture that offers human contact – life and movement – instead of the desolation that characterized Skärholmen. According to Bengtzon, the town center would have been able to offer an "all-round social service" and a "square full of life" if architects had shown greater concern for everyday life instead of single-mindedly prioritizing commercial demands. Above all, they should have "accepted" the Swedish climate and therefore built an indoor center;
 a roof over Skärholmen center would have made it possible to create a livelier and more congenial environment.[29]

The view that a roof over Skärholmen would have created a livelier and more human environment was shared by Bengtzon's colleague Clas Brunius. He compared Skärholmen center with another, similar complex in the suburban municipality of Täby, and observed that the inhabitants of Skärholmen were strikingly taciturn, while the atmosphere in Täby center was reminiscent of that in the market-hall in Florence:

29 Olle Bengtzon: "Skärholmens centrum – en uppvisning av svenskt överflöd," in: *Expressen,* 06.09.1968. Rebecka Tarschys also called department stores "temples"; "the Domus temple" is how she describes the Domus department store in Skärholmen, in "Skärholmen klart – nya mänskligare tag," in: *Dagens Nyheter,* 04.09.1968.

> "It's full of life. Conversation and laughter mix with happy sounds from the music stand. It's nice and warm under the roof. There are no doors to keep you out of the shops. The library is open, with a display of freshly-picked mushrooms from the area. [...] It's a place where street life flourishes."[30]

Advertising for Täby center also highlighted the free activities on offer. Visitors were invited to leave their coats at the reception, and enjoy "all-year-round summer warmth," admire the greenery "in a pleasant environment," while the children enjoyed the playground. There were "moving pavements" between the different levels, and free parking spaces outside.[31] The fact that visitors had no need to buy anything in order to take part in the life of Täby center was of key importance for Brunius' positive attitude. The opposite was true of Skärholmen; there, women and pensioners stood outside in the cold wind, silently gazing at the goods in the shop windows.[32]

A Light in the Darkness: Gallery-Access Houses

In the Skärholmen debate, gallery-access houses were seen as a light in the darkness that was Skärholmen. "People feel at home in these houses," wrote Olle Bengtzon, and went on: "The communal galleries give rise to natural contact between both children and adults." He made this claim in an otherwise negative article about Skärholmen with the title "Skärholmen, a Terrible Indictment."[33] Access galleries were generally seen in the 1960s as social spaces and meeting places. They were also regarded by many in the profession as an expression of structuralism, a theory within the social sciences that attracted great interest at that time.[34]

30 Clas Brunius: "Skärholmen? Nej! Täby? Ja!," in: *Expressen*, 30.09.1968.

31 Advertisement för Täby center in *Svenska Dagbladet*, 26.09.1968.

32 Brunius: "Skärholmen? Nej! Täby? Ja!"

33 Olle Bengtzon: "Skärholmen, en ohygglig anklagelse," in: *Expressen*, 18.06.1970.

34 One architect who often made use of access galleries in his projects was Ralph Erskine – for example, several years before the Skärholmen debate, in his design for the nationally-known Brittgården in Tibro. When the project was presented in architectural journals, the authors of the articles were unanimous in agreeing that access galleries promoted social communication. See the articles "Brittgården i Tibro" in the Danish journal *Arkitektur*, no. 5, 1966, pp. 200-207, and "Tibro" and "Angående Tibro" in the Swedish journal *Arkitektur*, no. 6, 1965, pp. 167-170 and pp. 172-179.

Skärholmen was much too far from the metro, said the critics. It was impossible for a housewife who wanted to break out of her isolation (!) to spend a few spare hours during the day visiting the National Museum, for instance, even though the metro journey itself only took 20 minutes. The walk from her home to the metro station was so long that it made a journey into the center of Stockholm considerably more difficult. Ulf Hård af Segerstad claims that her freedom to develop herself was restricted because the planners of Skärholmen had given too little consideration to women's everyday circumstances.[35] The solution would have been to build a linear town,[36] a type of design centered around a linear communication route. If the plan for Skärholmen and the surrounding neighborhoods had followed this ideal, it would have meant shorter walking distances for the inhabitants. During the time that had elapsed between the planning and building of Skärholmen, the widespread idea of new towns divided into neighborhoods had become unfashionable. It had been superseded by the kind of plan popularized by, among others, the planners of Hook New Town (London County Council, 1961), a British town that was never actually built, but nevertheless achieved world fame. As well as having a linear center, it was densely built up, with traffic segregation in the vertical dimension; instead of parking spaces at ground level outside the central complex, they were put in the basement. In this way, the architects freed up space for housing alongside the center, which helped to reduce walking distances. Brasilia, the new capital of Brazil, was also linear, as were a number of other contemporary projects in Europe. It is often the case in debates about architecture and town-planning that the built environment is loaded with strong connotations, either negative or positive, which overshadow nuances. In line with this tendency, Skärholmen came to be regarded not only as out-of-date but also unsuitable and even harmful, not least because of the long walking distances; short walking distances were regarded as an expression of planning suited to people's everyday lives.

35 Ulf Hård af Segerstad: "Från Skärholmen till Nationalmuseum," in: *Svenska Dagbladet*, 11.01.1968.

36 Ulf Hård af Segerstad: "Skärholmen som våra barnbarns slum," in: *Svenska Dagbladet*, 1.11.1968. Thomas Michélsen: "Från Skärholmen till Järva," in: *Dagens Nyheter*, 20.11.1968.

Inhabitants – Victims of an Unequal Distribution of Power

The Skärholmen debate was to focus largely on those groups in society to whom the critics believed the architects had paid too little attention. Women, children, pensioners, low wage-earners, and the disabled were among such groups mentioned, for example, by Thomas Michelsén in *Dagens Nyheter.* He thought Skärholmen probably functioned very well for healthy, high-earning car-owners, but hardly for other groups such as the low-waged, "the carless," the elderly, and the disabled.[37] Skärholmen was anti-egalitarian.

The fact that in the midst of prosperity there were groups and individuals who had not benefited from the rises in real income was a focus of discussion during the 1960s, and this is reflected not only in Michelsén's contributions but those of many other commentators, too. This was connected with the observations of left-wing intellectuals in the 1960s that there were oppositions within society.[38] There were people in the welfare state who could be defined as poor.[39] A similar discussion was under way in Great Britain at the same time.[40] The concern that critics in the Skärholmen debate showed for women, children, the low-waged, and other groups can in other words be understood as an expression of the contemporary criticism directed at society's inability to create equality, that is to say welfare and freedom of choice for all.

Equality is a matter of power. In contributions to the Skärholmen debate, there was a tacit ambition to reveal the power relations that favor certain groups but disadvantage others. The inhabitants, whom critics regarded as victims of an unequal distribution

37 Michelsén: "Från Skärholmen till Järva." Concern for disadvantaged groups became a typical feature of the times. Lars Gyllensten presents similar arguments in two published articles on urban architecture in general: "Arkitektur och samhälle," in: *Dagens Nyheter,* 24.09.1968, and in one on the rebuilding of Stockholm's city center: "Samhällsplanering – teknik eller politik," in: *Dagens Nyheter,* 26.09.1968. Elderly people, children and youths, the sick, and the disabled were citizens who had been disadvantaged, he believed, when the town was planned for "healthy, young, well-off car-owners."

38 Pål Strandbakken: "Det konfliktteoretiska alternativet till functionalism," in: Andersen and Kaspersen: *Klassisk och modern samhällsteori,* pp. 344-349.

39 Göran Therborn: "Arbetarrörelsen och välfärdsstaten," in: *Arkiv för arbetarrörelsens historia,* no. 41/42, 1989, pp. 3-51, p. 24.

40 Dennis Hardy: *From New Towns to Green Politics,* London: E and FN Spon, 1991, p. 6, pp. 63-94.

of power, were highlighted in the debate. The interests of these groups, it was said, had been given low or zero priority among those who had planned the development of Skärholmen. This view can be exemplified by an article in which Ulf Hård af Segerstad criticizes the tower blocks on the terrace above the center. He calls them "a vision seen from the E4."[41] He implies that the blocks were not built for the inhabitants, who according to Olle Bengtzon suffered from unhappiness and isolation. Instead, the architects had prioritized the need of motorists for visual stimulation; when they drove along Skärholmsvägen at high speed they could nevertheless catch a glimpse of the grandiose buildings on the terrace by the center. The blocks were there to catch the motorist's eye, and the price, according to Bengtzon, was paid by their inhabitants, who lived in blocks built on an "inhuman" scale on a "bare concrete deck."[42] This is one of a number of expressions of the unequal society that Skärholmen represented.

The "power analyses" critics conducted in the context of the debate also revealed that children were the victims of the unequal distribution of power. They were "strangled in their opportunities to develop," one psychologist believed.[43] Skärholmen was not designed with their needs in mind. One key problem was that they had nothing to do; they were inactive and lacked stimulation,[44] a claim that possibly suggests its author was unaware that Skärholmen had plenty of open-air recreation areas, woodland, football pitches, and play parks. One welfare officer says of the children in Skärholmen that: "Many of them are like the concrete that surrounds them – hard and distrustful." According to this source, the children have become so impaired that they cannot be reached by conventional treatment methods. The situation in Skärholmen, the reader of the article is given to understand, was so extraordinary that even the experts were at a loss as what to do; Skärholmen produced a type of person who had difficulty in making contact with others, and who was emotionally cold and introverted.[45]

Women represented another vulnerable group in Skärholmen. They were isolated, resigned to their fate and lonely, and they had no opportunity to develop themselves.

41 Ulf Hård af Segerstad: "Skärholmen som våra barnbarns slum," in: *Svenska Dagbladet*, 1.01.1968.

42 Olle Bengtzon: "Skärholmen, en ohygglig anklagelse," in: *Expressen*, 18.06.1970.

43 Gange Rolf: "Barnet verkar strypt," in: *Dagens Nyheter*, Sydväst, 25.06.1969.

44 Åsa Moberg: "Hemmafru i Skärholmen," in: *Aftonbladet*, 30.08.1968.

45 Ann Toreskog: "Så blir barnen som lever i förorternas stenöknar," in: *Expressen*, 17.06.1970.

The gloominess of women's existence led to a rise in alcohol problems; Skärholmen "turned women into secret drinkers," as *Aftonbladet* put it.[46] A woman says she would like to go on a course to learn something, but there are no courses in Skärholmen. The meager social environment contrasts with the physical: the super-modern laundry and the new furniture in the flat. The subtext of the article is that the high material standard of living is paid for by women; men are never at home, since they are constantly working to pay for all these luxuries.[47]

Equality and Service

The Skärholmen debate expressed currents of thought that were prevalent in the 1960s, not least the idea of equality, including equality between the sexes. Women's often unfree choice to "work at home" was noted increasingly in the early 1960s. Gender roles were to be the major topic of debate in the following years.[48] One contribution to the debate was the so-called low-income commission, appointed in 1965. The commission showed that many women had so much housework to do that it was difficult or impossible for them to combine it with employment. Housework was not a free choice, but forced women to stay at home, regardless of whether they wished to do so or not.[49] The commission also showed that there were large income differentials in the suburbs, perhaps bigger than had generally been imagined. One of the groups with low incomes, or none whatsoever, was women.[50]

One way to enable women to take up employment was for society to offer support services to the family. This was by no means a new idea. Blocks of service flats had,

46 Margareta Garpe: "Skärholmen tvingar fruarna att smygsupa," in: *Aftonbladet,* 23.09.1968.

47 Åsa Moberg: "Hemmafru i Skärholmen," in: *Aftonbladet* 30.08.1968. Similar criticisms were leveled at Bredäng. "It's a gradual death of the soul" say women in this suburb, according to Ulf Anzelius in "Förortstristess i Bredäng," in: *Dagens Nyheter,* Sydväst, 25.09.1968.

48 Kjell Östberg: 1968. *När allting var i rörelse,* Stockholm: Prisma, 2002, pp. 49-50.

49 Göran Ahrne: *Hushållsarbete och dubbelarbete, Utkast till kapitel 8 i betänkandet om svenska folkets levnadsförhållanden i Låginkomstutredningen,* Stockholm: Allmänna förlag, 1971.

50 Per Holmberg and Holger Ström: *Välstånd med slagsida. Låginkomstutredningens första betänkande i sammandrag,* Stockholm: Allmänna förlag, 1970.

earlier, been provided with restaurants and day nurseries, making it possible for both parents to work. In Sweden, service flats were the subject of a number of reports, in which their advantages were often emphasized.[51] Among representatives for the state and its municipalities, however, there was little interest, so that there was relatively little construction of collective housing in Sweden, not least because the high level of service was considered to be too expensive.[52]

In the light of the rise in real incomes in the 1950s and 1960s, the costs that might be involved in an increased commitment to public services came to be seen as reasonable. One driving force was the women's movement, which contributed to putting the concept of equality high on the agenda. Women's rights to employment and individual development were taken more seriously, especially the demand for childcare. Furthermore, the housewife ideal yielded to the needs of the employment market; this is at least how many people interpreted the parliamentary resolution on a substantial extension childcare of 1963. During the first half of the 1960s, representatives of the labor market campaigned to encourage women into employment. Newspapers published positively-loaded articles about working women, and Swedish radio produced a series of programs entitled "The Housewife Changes Jobs" ("Hemmafrun byter yrke").[53]

Service Becomes a Subject for Research

In 1967, the government appointed a committee with the task of considering problems in the area of housing and services. The term "services" was taken to include whatever lightened the burden of housework and provided increased opportunities for activities to develop the personality. Childcare, care of the elderly, the sick and the

51 Sven Markelius was among those who assumed that tower blocks with communal facilities to make housework easier would become usual in the future. Sven Markelius: "Människan i centrum?," in: *Plan*, no. 1/2, 1950, pp. 47-53.

52 Brita Åkerman: *88 år på 1900-talet*, Stockholm: Fischer, 1994, pp. 163-164 and "Hemmen och samhällsplaneringen," SOU 1956: 32, p. 9.

53 Östberg: 1968. *När allting var i rörelse*, pp. 49-50.

disabled, and leisure services, i.e., premises with organized activities (comparable with civic halls) were included, as were cleaning and cooking, which could be offered to households.[54] New state and municipal rent allowances enabled less well-off families to move into flats with a high level of services.[55]

Social service became a way of creating an equitable society with a high standard of living for all. The concept of service took on almost as great an importance as the concept of equality. Equality was not only a matter of gender. Every aspect that might have a negative impact on the individual's development prospects, and inhibit their freedom of choices and options was taken into account: class, age, disability, etc. By providing housing services, society contributed to raising living standards, especially for those groups whose opportunities were severely restricted without such services.

The concept of service was used not only by state researchers but also by architects, judging by the fact that their own journal *Arkitektur* dealt with the concept several times. Walkways inside buildings or covered passages, short walking distances and a high level of service, including staffed receptions, became the ideal in the latter half of the 1960s, as is evident from the Skärholmen debate, from the architects' own journal *Arkitektur,* and from other publications.[56]

The Egalitarian Town of Norra Järva

Entries for the competition for the development of the Norra Järva new town in 1967
show that the ideals described above were also established among practicing architects. The competitors emphasized the concept of service. Walkways inside buildings or covered passages were common elements in the entries, so that the residents could move easily and conveniently between the dwellings and the various service facilities. "New-old town" was a term used in the competition's winning entry, meaning integration, compactness, life, and movement. Gallery-access houses were common in

54 "Boendeservice 1," SOU 1968: 38, p. 9.

55 "Boendeservice 1," SOU 1968: 38, p. 78.

56 "Höga eller låga hus," SOU 1967: 30, p. 117.

the entries, as well as tower blocks.[57] It can be added that the Järva competition was judged a year before the start of the Skärholmen debate, so it was not the case that Skärholmen acted as a watershed.

The buildings of Norra Järva were designed around a pedestrian zone. It is, in other words, a linear town. The main thoroughfare is not built-in, but parts of it are covered by a roof. The ideal solution would have been to create an "indoor street," but in Norra Järva, and in many other cases, the planners made do with a roof to offer protection against strong sunshine and rain, and heating in the street surface to melt snow and ice. Cultural and commercial services are concentrated along the thoroughfare in Norra Järva, along with the metro, which has two entrances at each station in order to minimize walking distances, and day nurseries, "meeting points," and schools, which were also intended for the inhabitants to use after school hours for meetings, courses, etc.

By removing services and meeting places to the main communication route, which was within easy reach of everyone, this plan, along with the high level of services, contributed towards equality. Groups, which, without support, had limited opportunities to shape their lives as they wished, would achieve a higher standard of living with the service offered by Norra Järva; for instance women, if they had small children, needed childcare to be able to work, and many elderly people needed day-to-day help if they were to be able to choose where they lived. If services were not provided, they were forced into care homes. Interpreted in this way, the plan is an expression of a politically critical architecture. It aims to reform an unequal society.

Alongside the central thoroughfare, there are blocks of flats, including gallery-access houses. This type of housing, praised in the Skärholmen debate, was built in large quantities in Norra Järva. Between the houses there are playgrounds and sports fields, hobby workshops, day nurseries, and so on. There are also low-rise blocks of flats and terrace houses made available to rent. Rentable terrace houses can be seen as an answer to the criticism that people with low incomes had to live in flats, even though many of them, according to a number of studies, expressed a wish to live in a self-contained house. Even though a large number of terraced and detached houses had been built in

57 *Arkitekttävlingar*, no. 3, 1967, "Järvafältet," pp. 81-110.

the 1950s and 1960s, they were not normally available for rent. The compact, low-rise areas of rentable terrace houses can thus be interpreted as a reflection of the debate about the unequal society.

Architects and building firms were in charge, while the "users", as people were called around 1970, were powerless; this was how the criticism of inequality in this area was widely interpreted. Modern architecture was elitist, liked by architects but disliked by the general public. The architectural style that came into vogue during the 1970s, in Akalla and elsewhere, could be interpreted as a consequence of this criticism. Allowing terrace house architecture to go back to the designs of Swedish peasant culture enabled the creation of a more egalitarian relationship between the profession and the users. Here, architects showed that they had something to learn from a folk tradition.

To a large extent, in the planning and in the resulting built environment, Norra Järva is an expression of the ideals that the critics of Skärholmen advocated. Norra Järva had features that were lacking in Skärholmen. But the two developments also had certain things in common. They were both new towns with workplaces, housing, and commercial and cultural facilities. They both had educational institutions, health care, and other social services, even if the social services in Norra Järva were regarded as more comprehensive. They both date from approximately the same time, as is reflected in their architectural design. They both follow the principle of traffic segregation and they are both situated in environmentally attractive areas: Skärholmen on the shores of Lake Mälaren and Norra Järva adjacent to a captivating and varied natural landscape with, among other features, extensive rambling areas, three lakes, over 1,000 hectares of forest, open land, and older buildings in the form of farms and cottages from the eighteenth and nineteenth centuries.[58]

Both Skärholmen and Norra Järva were planned as independent towns in many respects, if not in all, and this entailed planning for the establishment of businesses. The business zone in Kista in Norra Järva became one of the most successful, not just in Sweden but in the whole world. In the 1980s, because the computer industry was concentrated here, it became known as Sweden's Silicon Valley. In an international comparison, Kista has been found to have the world's fifth-greatest concentration of

58 Jan-Erik Tomth: *Att bo i Norra Järva*, Stockholm: Utrednings- och statistikkontoret, 1984, p. 192.

IT firms.[59] This status is reflected in a number of prestigious and architectonically exclusive office blocks. Communications are excellent, with short journey times to Arlanda airport as well as to the center of Stockholm.

Social Problems and Design

Happy working mothers with access to a high level of services did not become the symbol of Norra Järva, which had short walking distances, good services, gallery-access houses, and rentable terrace houses. On the contrary, it had to fight a battle against the label "problem area." During the 1970s, as the town gradually took shape, new towns were generally presented in the media as failures, dirty, and untidy. The pictures were dominated by social outcasts and criminals. Ten years later, the residents were still a problem group, this time because of their ethnic origin.[60]

Today's debate concerns the ethnic segregation and poverty in some of the new towns; the inhabitants have a relatively low average income. In some sectors of the town-planning profession, it is claimed that this state of affairs is a result of the physical planning of the new towns, and that they should therefore be rebuilt. The principle of building new towns divided into neighborhood units creates isolation, it is said. Traffic segregation, which was ultimately intended to create a better living environment, especially for children, is today seen as a hindrance to economic development. There is a belief that through traffic generates enterprise and trade, but also security, according to Swedish architects who, in the early 1990s, discovered Jane Jacobs' *The Death and Life of Great American Cities* (1961). Inspired by this book, which deals with the situation in New York at the end of the 1950s, they claim that the built environments of the 1960s and 1970s, which are planned so as to exclude through

59 From Johan Rittsél: "Kista," in: Söderström and Jermsten: *Stockholm utanför tullarna,* pp. 354-359, p. 359.

60 Urban Ericsson, Irene Molina, and Per-Markku Ristilammi: *Miljonprogram och media. Föreställningar om människor och förorter,* Stockholm: Riksantikvarieämbetet, 2002, p. 18. It is important to remember that there are some districts that are rarely or never mentioned in such discussions from this period, whereas other areas recur constantly.

traffic as far as possible, are wrongly constructed. With a different type of street plan, people from immigrant backgrounds, who find it difficult to gain a foothold in the job market, would be able to create their own job opportunities by developing businesses, the critics say. Perhaps implicit in this view of the need for streets is the notion that small businesses owned by people with immigrant backgrounds are synonymous with the sale of pizzas and sweets, i.e., the restaurant and retail trades, which tend to be located in streets or squares with large numbers of passers-by.[61]

Architects believe, therefore, that the design of the street network has a decisive influence on social problems such as ethnic and economic segregation. We only need to rebuild problem areas, build new streets and reduce the space taken up by park areas, and allow residents to buy properties, so they say, and there will be better integration and enterprise will flourish. The last point is crucial, because when the towns came into being, according to the stories being circulated today, there was no provision made for employment. This is, as we have seen, an erroneous assertion (think of Kista, for example) and illustrates the commentators' lack of knowledge of the places they have set themselves up as experts on.

Regardless of what the ambitions of the new town critics are – political, social, or careerist – systematic criticism of the new towns will clearly not promote either integration or economic development.[62] Those who wish to contribute to a positive development should, in my view, find other ways of doing so, rather than using models of town-planning that are fashionable today as the basis for criticizing what was built yesterday.

61 A change of ownership is also on the agenda; a sale of public housing is recommended. The account given of these criticisms is based on a number of articles by Jerker Söderlind in which he criticizes the new towns. The illustrations here are from three articles, from 2001, 2004, and 2005. In the 2004 article, the towns are called "ghettos" and described in terms of isolation and desolation. The author argues consistently that both the physical design and the form of ownership need changing. He cites as his basis for the latter view an article in *Göteborgsposten* by two politicians, of the Social Democratic and Moderate parties. See Jerker Söderlind: "En arkitekts försvarstal," in: *Dagens Nyheter,* 20.06.2001; Jerker Söderlind, Tigran Hasic et al.: "Så kan Tensta förvandlas" (with the introduction "Blås liv i gettona"), in: *Svenska Dagbladet,* 9.12.2004; Jerker Söderlind: "ABC för Stockholm," in: *Stockholm den växande staden,* Stockholm: Samfundet Sankt Eriks Årsbok, 2005, pp. 116-125.

62 This was noted earlier by Ericsson, Molina and Ristilammi: *Miljonprogram och media.*

Positive Expectations and Undreamed Possibilities

It should be possible to investigate the positive aspects of the environments in question, not only their limitations. If, for example, I accept the idea that it would be a good thing if more businesses were established in the new towns, I could ask how many of the inhabitants have training and/or experience in fields other than the restaurant and retail trades, activities, which, according to the debate, require a different type of town from the one that actually exists. Perhaps the inhabitants' skills extend over a number of areas such as the information and service sectors, manufacturing and workshop industries, horticulture or food production, to name but a few that would not require any rebuilding of the street network. The new towns already have industrial zones with premises suitable for firms.

The local community can perhaps make a positive contribution, rather than function solely as a limiting factor. Inhabitants who start and run firms can become local celebrities in a neighborhood unit or a small town (a place described in negative terms as an isolated enclave): people who are seen on their way to or from work, in the shops, at a parents' meeting, in the park or the swimming pool. They can pass on their experience, build networks, and by their mere presence serve as an inspiration to others.

Nature, with all the possibilities it offers for recreation and play, can also be seen as a resource and not, as in today's debate, as a problem. Jane Jacobs' theory that parks have a divisive and isolating effect because people do not want to be in them after dusk, should, I think, be weighed against the positive influence of parks and other green areas during the daytime. Anyone who suggested, for example, that Hampstead Heath in London should be built on, for the reasons put forward by Jacobs, would almost certainly meet with resistance. The inhabitants of this part of London generally value the open space. In Stockholm, some architects say exactly the same of the unbuilt area of Norra Järva. The natural surroundings are among the things most valued by the inhabitants, who do not, therefore, share the view that nature is a problem.[63] It remains to be seen how much resistance they can offer.

63 Tomth: *Att bo i Norra Järva*, p. 192.

The well-developed social, cultural, and commercial facilities (there are apparently between 130 and 140 shops in Kista and in Skärholmens centrum); the traffic-free, child-friendly, and quiet residential areas; the well-equipped playgrounds; the good communications; swimming-pools, riding schools and sports facilities – these are other assets.

I finish by quoting the American sociologist Richard Senneth, who in the 1990s visited Hallunda/Norsborg, a part of Botkyrkastaden, which was developed around 1970. Standing in front of a block of flats and its courtyard, green with vegetation, he shouted out: "These are your problem areas?! Is there an empty apartment? I'll move in right away!"[64]

About the author

Lisbeth Söderqvist, Ph D, is currently research officer at the Scientific Council for Humanities and Social Sciences in Stockholm. She is a Swedish architectural historian with a special interest in the 1950s, 1960s, and 1970s. She has written a number of books and articles in which she discusses architecture and urban planning in the context of the development of the European welfare state, for example: *Rekordår och miljonprogram: flerfamiljshus i stor skala: en fallstudiebaserad undersökning av politik, planläggning och estetik* (1999) on city planning and *Att gestalta välfärd: från idé till byggd miljö* (2008) on the development of Swedish and European cities between 1945 and 1975.

64 Professor Richard Sennett was taking part in a seminar which included an excursion to a residential area. It was organized by the Multicultural Center in Fittja, Stockholm, on the initiative of Professor Karl-Olof Arnstberg (1995/96).

"... BUT IT WAS BASED ON AN IDEA OF MINE!"

MODERN ART, MODERNISM, AND THE HANSAVIERTEL – STILL CONNECTED TO THE NORTH

Matthias Ot

On the occasion of the fiftieth anniversary of the Interbau international building exhibition in Berlin, we brought to fruition the project "Echtzeitsehen <) stadtfinden_moderne."[1] The basis of the project was a concept questioning contemporary appreciation of the architecture in the Hansaviertel in Berlin and exploring individual possibilities of access to the modern ideas in the year 2007. At the same time, a new technology, which in 2007 could still claim avant-garde status, was exploited to revive the old architectural exhibition: with the aid of GPS-equipped pocket computers, visitors to the exhibition could move freely throughout the neighborhood while receiving multimedia information relating to the real urban environment at almost a hundred "points of interest."

In developing the content, a type of observer or visitor to this aging group of buildings fundamentally different to the exhibition visitor of 1957 was the point of departure. Perhaps the most conspicuous characteristic of today's visitor is his strongly individualistic tendency, his detachment from and skepticism towards the acceptance of collective traditions, and the trend towards personal assimilation of the architectural or social heritage by means of concise, visual ideas, which in their medial affinity often barely require differentiation from city tourism marketing material. In dealing with the zeitgeist, it seemed appropriate to track down such visual ideas or labels which could be both less easy to abridge as well as taken in by the individual in total privacy, and to approach this state of affairs in an ironic, creative, and – where applicable – provocative way.

Reference to a common heritage, be it modern or otherwise, in our society is thus not in keeping with the zeitgeist. This may not least be due to the availability of communication technology for the individual, which leads to a general supremacy of esthetics – and in large part has become an esthetic of and for self-promotion. To face such individuals prepared, it may well be appropriate to heed the workings of the "economy of attention" all the way to "mental capitalism"[2] and reflect on a dominant

1 Supported by the Capital Cultural Fund. See also http://www.hauptstadtkulturfonds.berlin.de/index.php?id=132 [available 10.06.09].

2 See Georg Franck: *Ökonomie der Aufmerksamkeit*, Munich: Hanser, 1998 and "Mental capitalism," in: *What People Want. Populism in Architecture and Design;* ed. Michael Shamiyeh and DOM Research Laboratory; Basel, Boston, and Berlin: Birkhäuser, 2005, pp. 98-115.

"culture of narcissism."[3] These processes of subjective reception, opposed to many of the modern age's notions of the individual and virtually the reversal of certain approaches such as "social engineering,"[4] are also significant for the perception of architecture:

> For things and symbols, the *via regia* into subjective experience is their promise that consuming them will make the consumer irresistible. It is clear that in a society where attention income becomes a major objective, consumption will follow the pull of self-esteem.[5]

From this perspective, the modern age as an epoch is only too gladly reduced to a handful of names, as if it consisted of individual and appropriable achievements: this furniture by Henry Clement van de Velde, this lamp by Arne Jacobsen, that teapot by Alvar Aalto. Objects become labels with which the individual of today is happy to adorn himself. If they come from 1957, they are furthermore termed "retro styles." Modern designers and architects appear as stars of good taste.

With other names, however, this attitude stops short and provokes stubborn reactions. Corbusier? "Those enormous concrete monstrosities?" Gropius? "Dull satellite towns?" Or Fisker? Samuelson? "Does anyone still know them today?" The Hansaviertel in Berlin? "The prefabs of the West!" Here, a somewhat uncomfortable reality is forcibly recalled: that modern architecture might not only owe something to taste but that for a good part it consisted of a concept related to society. The observer of today cannot assimilate this aspect individually. It is something people participated in – and still participate in – collectively. Insofar as the zeitgeist cannot or will not understand this anymore, it sees the modern age (or the postwar modern age, as in the case of the Hansaviertel) as simply solid concrete in the city landscape, for many people nothing other than a seemingly dry and immutable reality not even worth taking a snap of.

---

3 See Christopher Lasch: *The Culture of Narcissism*, New York: Warner Books, 1979.

4 See Karl Popper: *Die offene Gesellschaft und ihre Feinde*, Tübingen: Mohr, 1992.

5 Georg Franck: "Mentaler Kapitalismus," in: *Merkur*, vol. 57, no. 645, 2003, pp. 1-15.

Is there really no other idea that leads from today's individualist to the modern age? "No, I didn't build it myself. But it's based on an idea of mine"[6] – this motto was dedicated to the financial situation in the city of Berlin in 2005, in essence the management of an immense debt burden from the banking scandal of 2001, which could barely be shouldered by society any longer and had deviated far from the original ideas of a city treasurer. The Berlin Senate clearly felt the need to explain humorously how it could personally allegorize itself as a bulwark against the flood of debts to the individual of today: as a small beaver, thoroughly capable of irony, confronted with a gigantic dam.

For individual access to the societal heritage of the international building exhibition of 1957, it was just those Berlin fiscal policymakers who seemed to have found an apt image: a magnificent monument of functionalism here casts its reinforced concrete shadow over the aged (social) housing of postwar modernism of a city, which after the fall of the wall in 1989 already seems to be seeking the protection of a new (embankment) wall. To better exploit the opportunities of this image given to the user of the GPS guide, we again moved and contained the projections surfaces: the positive protective function of functionalist buildings for the general public or the label of working modern society were combined with the "Nordic model," as it was and is gladly perceived in Germany as hackneyed.

The beaver position – insistence on the property of ideas on a small scale – was associated with fine artists and, to maintain a relationship to the Nordic architecture in the Hansaviertel, specifically young artists from Iceland, Finland, Sweden, Denmark, and Norway.

6 This quotation comes from the financial budget for Berlin from 2005 to 2009. The Berlin financial budget is perhaps the clearest reminder of the situation in public budgets across Germany. A constantly and rapidly growing mountain of debt can only be eased cosmetically by one's own efforts. The prospect of a financial future without external help does not exist: "in his 'Nobel lecture,' given on 8 December 2008, Jack S. Kilby, co-inventor of the principle of integrated circuits, cites Nobel Prize winner Charles Townes with a story of a beaver and a rabbit staring transfixed at the Hoover Dam; in the end, the beaver agrees to the statement: 'No, I didn't build it myself. But it's based on an idea of mine.' The image of a dam and yet more of its breach in relation to public debt has long since found its way into the politico-economic debate."

In turn, the artistic position is very compatible with the zeitgeist. Berlin – "poor but sexy"[7] – is also the new art metropolis. For all artists and those involved in the artistic sector, whether poor or rich, established or a nobody, Berlin has become the most attractive hub for art and culture in recent years. However, if Berlin-based artists profit from the rather involuntary financial "avant-garde role" of the city, if they can work on their ideas all the more creatively because their activity falls under the shadow of threatening dam breaches, the question may also be put of whether here an esthetic is dealing with the social architecture of the metropolis in an entirely free and arbitrary way, or whether the artists are not by any chance confronting such urbanist legacies such as the cemented utopias of the Western postwar era (and also those of socialism in the East) in a more productive way. And indeed! After it was rather the half-deserted/half-dilapidated inner-city neighborhoods of (East) Berlin that formed the artist's playground in the 1990s, since the turn of the millennium, more modern stock is gradually becoming the focus of attention.

Unusually, many Scandinavians are to be found among the artists today coming to Berlin in droves. At the same time, an above average number of those who were inspired by Interbau and actually constructed buildings came from northern Europe. The presentation of a by all means meaningful encounter thus appeared all the more interesting: were ideas worked out here with esthetic means of expression based on a social discourse of modernism as was conducted in an exemplary way in northern Europe? With the buildings by Fisker, Aalto, Samuelson, and Jacobsen, there are both the tangible reference objects in the Hansaviertel as well as constructed visual demonstrations of the Nordic visionaries in their response to the modern utopia of the 1950s. Here, the background of the individual architects is also always illuminated, i.e., the status and development of what for years was the defining element in Germany in its gaze northwards: the "Nordic model." We therefore sought cooperation with the neighboring Nordic embassies, resulting in the symposium entitled "Das nordische Modell und die Moderne," curated by Caroline Spliid Høgsbro. However,

7 Klaus Wowereit, Mayor of Berlin, first made this connection in an interview for the magazine FOCUS-Money in November 2003. He was asked "Does money make you sexy?" and answered by rejecting a connection between erotic magnetism and wealth: "No. You can see that in Berlin. We may be poor, but we're still sexy."

access to a "modern understanding" of the architecture in the Hansaviertel with the aid of its Nordic backdrop was not to be liberated from the wiles of current and individualistic perception. As a result, "Stadtfinden Moderne" did not excessively touch on (historical) information on the Nordic societies but attempted to trace the presence of a contemporary conception of modernism in just those young Nordic artists who today work in Berlin. Thus Iceland and Norway, although they are not represented at Interbau, were allocated two "Points of Interest" each in a special "Nordic Line."

A detailed verbal account of the various artistic standpoints would be beyond the scope of this anthology. In general, however, one common feature can be summarized: confronting modern forms and even the traditional social environment as an artistic collection of sources coalesces with the working principles of the artists Elmgreen&Dragset, Miklos Gaal, Ola Kolehmainen, Osmo Rauhala, Elin Hansdottir&Darri Lorenzen, Erla Haraldsdottir, Lars O. Ramberg, Soile Lahdenperäa, and Anna-Maija Terävä. An exemplary case is presented by the 2003 "Meldeamt" installation by Elmgreen&Dragset, which thematizes the waiting room in a registration office. Something which seems unexpectedly familiar, in the shadow of modern tower blocks. Of course: societies that do not have such bureaucratic apparatuses are regrettable and antiquated. And yet, the untroubled, gray waiting, interrupted only by occasional call numbers that have already fallen to the floor, is nothing that can enthuse us about our modern achievements, but rather something like a "critical idyll."

In this way, however, one certain question will hopefully repeatedly find its way back into the discussions our societies must conduct: which style is appropriate for us, if we want to be remembered as a – like it or not – "modern society"? Or, in the words of Rem Koolhaas: "Architecture should serve content and structures. 'How do we want to live? What possibilities does modernism open up for us?'"[8]

8 From the *Berlin Programm* from February (p. 9), with noae of a *Rem-Koolhaas-Lecture* at the Renaissance Theatre in Berlin on 1 February 2009, Rimbach Verlag Berlin.

159

About the author

Mathias Ott is a cultural studies expert who works as a freelance copywriter, concept designer, and media designer. His most recent projects were *landvermesser.tv – Literatur&Stadt* (Berlin 2008-2009); *Stadtfinden_Moderne – 50 Jahre Interbau in 1957 Berlin*; the conceptual design *Skulpturensommer 2008* for the Verein Parkkultur Rügen; and *Saray Sosyal – Über die Repräsentationsfunktionen von Schlössern und Wohnburgen* (Berlin 2005), which was supported by the Capital Cultural Fund. He made the film *Greif zur Kamera!* on the cultural policy of the 'Bitterfelder Weg', and is an independent research assistant for the exhibition project 50 Jahre Kulturpalast Bitterfeld – Kulturpolitik der DDR at the Wilhelm-Fraenger-Institut, Berlin.

PHOTO ESSAY

HANSAVIERTEL AND VÄLLINGBY

Cover of the German magazine *Baumeister,* 1948.
The German architect is looking over the fence to Scandinavia and Switzerland for inspiration.

A total of 53 architects from 13 countries took part in the architectural competition for *Interbau* announced in 1952. 39 of the 48 planned contributions were realized, with four well-known Scandinavian architects represented: the Danes Arne Jacobsen and Kay Fisker, the Finn Alvar Aalto, the German-Swedish architects Fritz Jaenecke and Sten Samuelson. A Dane (Christian Theodor Sørensen) and a Swede (Edvard Jacobsen) were involved in the landscaping and garden architecture. The Finnish architect Eero Saarinen designed the furniture for the show apartment in the Gropius House.

Arne Jacobsen's teacher Kay Fisker (1893–1965) is credited with reconciling the stylistic influences of European modernism and the modest Danish architectural tradition. Fisker's three to four-story balcony access block indeed exhibits restrained dimensions (Bartningallee 10 A–D, 1958). The building process and the combination of the construction units are emphasized by the white cross walls which contrast with the dark gray paint of the façades. Fisker carried out numerous social housing construction projects; his design of the group of buildings of Aarhus University (1930–44) with Christian Frederik Møller has ensured him an established position in the Danish architectural canon.

Top: The eight-story building by Finnish architect Alvar Aalto (1898–1976) is reputed to be the most popular dwelling among residents in the Hansaviertel (Klopstockstraße 30–32). The lighting levels, considered harmonious and healthy, are primarily the result of the large apartment windows and their multiple orientations. The building's gentle hint of a rotation allows for optimal sun exposure. As the metaphorical center of the democratic nuclear family, the "Allraum" (central room) was staged as a meeting place.

Top: Arne Jacobsen's atrium houses on Händelallee 33 to 39 rank among the quiet sensations of the development. They are privately partitioned and feature prudent insulation against the noise of the Berlin thoroughfares which run through the green spaces of the Hansaviertel and the Tiergarten.

Left bottom: Arne Jacobsen's teacher Kay Fisker (1893-1965) is credited with reconciling the stylistic influences of European modernism and the modest Danish architectural tradition. Fisker's three to four-story balcony access block indeed exhibits restrained dimensions (Bartningallee 10 A-D, 1958). The building process and the combination of the construction units are emphasized by the white cross walls which contrast with the dark gray paint of the façades. Fisker carried out numerous social housing construction projects; his design of the group of buildings of Aarhus University (1930-44) with Christian Frederik Møller has ensured him an established position in the Danish architectural canon.

Vällingby:
Lantern on stairway leading from the library to the square. In recent years, Vällingby has been carefully restored with great attention to detail, revealing a tendency to nostalgic stylization of the 'folkhem'. The "Million Program" of the 1960s and 70s has not yet acquired this level of acceptance.

Vällingby Center:
Vällingby was built on the model of the ABC city: work areas (arbete), living areas (bostad), and shopping areas (centrum) were to be concentrated in one location, giving residents a feeling of independence from Stockholm city center. (Despite some rows of shops and the infrastructure at Hansaplatz, this desired autonomous status was not characteristic of the Hansaviertel). The famous square in Vällingby, with its circular, colored cobblestones and water fountain, presents an inviting view – sitting on a bench here, all the achievements of the modern world, from the cinema, via the library and shops, to the subway entrance, can be taken in.

Architecture model of the Interbau 57

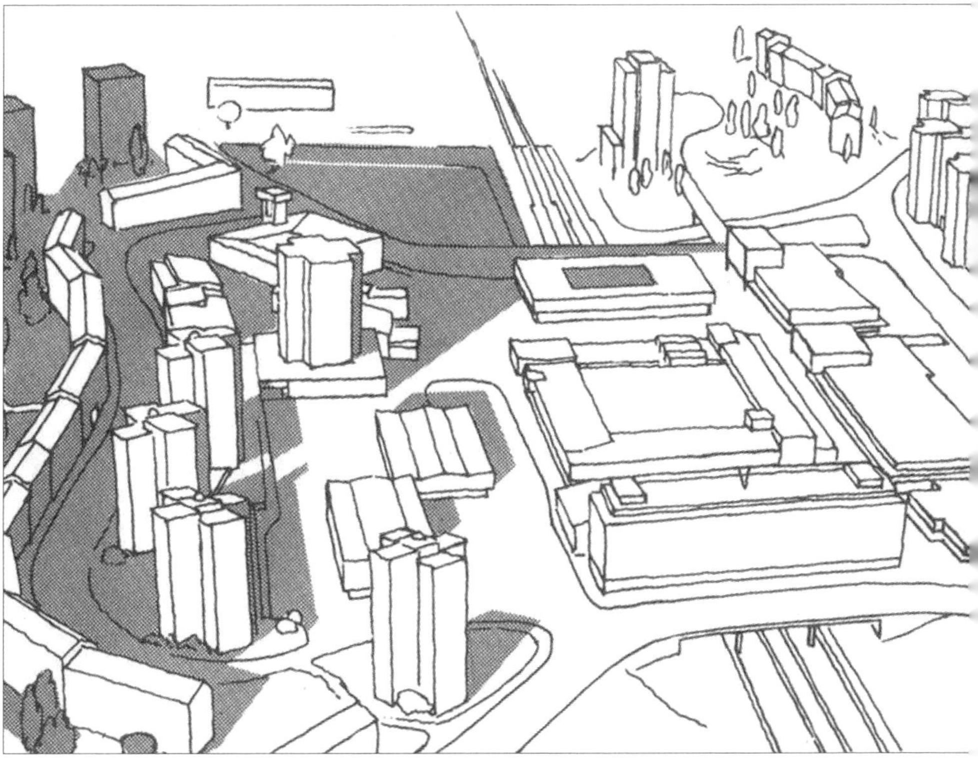

Draft of Vällingby

Bildnachweis

p 160 Cover of the German magazine Baumeister, November 1948

p 162 Postcard of Jaenecke/Samuelsson house at the Interbau

p 163 Jaenecke/Samuelsson at the Interbau / © Julieta Benito Sanz, 2007

p 164 t Alvar Aalto at the Interbau / © die stadt von morgen/Hermann Kondermann, 1957
b Kay Fisker at the Interbau / © Tim Schnetgöke

p 165 Arne Jacobsen at the Interbau after the conversion by Kirsten Schemel Architects, Berlin in 2005 / © Stefan Müller. Rights of use by Kirsten Schemel

p 166 Vällingby / © Antje Wischmann

p 168 Byggmästaren Tidskrift för arkitektur och byggnadsteknik, Stockholm, 1956 / © Lennart Olson, 1956

p 169 Vällingby Center / © Holger Ellgard, 2009

p 170 Architecture model of the Interbau 57 / © die stadt von morgen/Hermann Kondermann, 1957

p 171 Draft of Vällingby from the cover of: AB Svenska Bostäder: Vällingby, Stockholm: Roos Tryckerier, 1966

About the Editors

Caroline Spliid Høgsbro is a journalist. She studied architecture at the Technical University Berlin and film, media, and cultural studies at the University of Copenhagen; commissions for Danish newspapers, magazines on the subjects of architecture, culture, and Berlin history, screenwriter for Danish television TV2 and editor of the German magazine for design and architecture *H.O.M.E.* She designed the innovative exhibition concept Die Planrolle (a winner in the competition of the UIA World Congress of Architecture 2002) and curated and hosted the symposium "Das Nordische Modell und die Moderne" at the Nordic Embassies in Berlin in 2007.

Antje Wischmann is currently visiting professor in Scandinavian Studies at the University of Tübingen, lecturer at the Department for Northern European Studies at the Humboldt University Berlin, and research associate at Södertörn University in Stockholm; relevant publications: *Verdichtete Stadtwahrnehmung. Untersuchungen zum literarischen und urbanistischen Diskurs in Skandinavien 1955-95* (2003); *Auf die Probe gestellt – zur Debatte um die ‚neue Frau' der 1920er und 1930er Jahre in Schweden, Dänemark und Deutschland* (2006); publications in cultural and literary studies.

About the proofreader/translator

Oliver Dahin is a musicologist and translator. He studied at St Edmund Hall, Oxford University, before staying on to write a doctorate on the relationship between music and politics in the works of Hanns Eisler. Co-editor of the *Eisler-Studien* and editor for the new Eisler *Gesamtausgabe*. He has translated numerous academic texts and is currently working on a monograph on the Austrian composer and songwriter Fritz Spielmann, supported by the *Zukunftsfonds der Republik Österreich* and in association with the Academy of Arts in Berlin.

175

Acknowledgment

We thank the Nordic Embassies in Berlin for supporting the symposium that led to this book, Chrish Klose for her wonderful work and her patience, our proofreader and translator Oliver Dahin for his incredible thouroughness, the authors for sharing their work, our translators Jonathan Marks and Alexander Zuckrow, Berthold Fuchs for his support, Verena Harzer and stadtfinden_moderne: Mathias Ott and Tido von Oppeln for their inspiration and Södertörns Högskolas Library for their help with the research.

IMPRESSUM

TRANSLATION: Oliver Dahin, Jonathan Marks and Alexander Zuckrow
DESIGN AND SETTING: www.studiograu.de, Chrish Klose
PRINTING AND BINDING: fgb freiburger graphische betriebe

Mit freudlicher Unterstützung der
Königlich Dänische Botschaft Berlin

Bibliographic information published by Die Deutsche Bibliothek
Die Deutsche Bibliothek lists this publication in the Deutsche Nationalbibliografie; detailed bibliographic data are available on the Internet at http://dnb.ddb.de

jovis Verlag GmbH
Kurfürstenstraße 15/16
10785 Berlin

www.jovis.de
ISBN 978-3-86859-027-2